The Second Bookend

Completing a Life

SUSAN S. JORGENSEN

APPLECART PRESS

Book design by Brenda Klinger
Cover design by Amy H. Jorgensen
Copyediting by Jennifer Hanshaw Hackett
Proofreading by Maria Montesano Boyer

PRINTED IN THE UNITED STATES OF AMERICA

ISBN 978-0692638910

10 9 8 7 6 5 4 3 2 1

First Edition

Contents

FOREWORD 5

PROLOGUE 9

PART ONE: This Side of Home

CHAPTER ONE: Seeds of Change 15

CHAPTER TWO: Dying 31

CHAPTER THREE: Dead 51

CHAPTER FOUR: Bookends 69

CHAPTER FIVE: The Other Side of the Coin 79

CHAPTER SIX: Loss 93

CHAPTER SEVEN: Necessary and Natural 113

CHAPTER EIGHT: Completion and Beauty 127

CHAPTER NINE: Words 141

CHAPTER TEN: Conversations 159

CHAPTER ELEVEN: Compassion 173

CHAPTER TWELVE: Business 189

PART TWO: The Other Side of Home

CHAPTER THIRTEEN: Reflections 209

CHAPTER FOURTEEN: Dancing between the Thresholds 225

EPILOGUE 253

Foreword

As a spiritual director, Susan Jorgensen spent her professional life cultivating the art of being present with her clients and translating their subtle experiences into words. She used metaphors to capture the movement of an unfolding inner life and to support the ineffable sense of moving toward an intimate relationship with the Great Mystery. In *The Second Bookend,* she turns her studied attention to her personal experience of dying with the same presence and subtlety she gave to her clients for decades.

In this book, Susan emerges as a shockingly honest and soulful reporter facing her own death in her early sixties, a surprise event in an otherwise active and engaged life. She draws on the full force of her personal spiritual practice to meet death fully. Too soon, yet here and now, death arrives, and in these pages Susan does not shirk from this reality.

She completed *The Second Bookend* within a few months of her dying—she preferred the bluntness of accuracy rather than euphemisms like "passing away," which avoid the reality of death. Early on, as she told friends that she was dying, she met considerable resistance. They wanted her to have hope, to try an experimental drug or a new doctor—anything that would keep her alive. They didn't want to lose her. But Susan's own doctor told her the truth—her illness was terminal.

Susan was puzzled about her friends' reactions. "Don't they know the body dies?" she asked.

We have not evolved very far from fifty years ago, when psychiatrist Elisabeth Kübler-Ross asked her medical colleagues for referrals to patients who were dying in a large Chicago hospital. Amazingly, none of the medical doctors reported that they had any dying patients. Eventually, a man from the janitorial staff, having heard of her interest, directed Kübler-Ross to a woman who was dying in a certain room. This is how Kübler-Ross found her first dying patient to interview.

Although there is now a growing movement toward palliative and hospice care and death with dignity, most of our culture is still consumed with being young forever and fighting the good fight whenever illness arises. Toward the end of life, high-tech medicine seduces patients to gamble their remaining quality of life in hopes of a reprieve or cure, overestimating the chance of success. Neither they nor their doctors can face the grim reality of death.

Susan would have none of this. She insisted on talking about her upcoming death almost as if it were a long-planned vacation. Death, dying, terminal—these words came up around the dinner table between "Pass the veggies" and "More wine, please." She talked about sensing subtle help from the other side in the same way she talked about the visit from the hospice nurse. By necessity, her world was becoming smaller in concrete ways even as she was expanding into other realms, entering into the beyond.

Susan's terminal illness intensified the movement of her inner life to begin a new relationship with death. From a psychological point of view, she moved into the final stage of Jungian individuation, which she called completion. By either name, it's the process of becoming a whole human being through the reconciliation of opposites, as illustrated by her diagrams of overlapping circles. She reconciled the loss of leaving loved ones with the beauty of entering into the mystery of dying. She grieved even as she found a way to relate to death as a natural part of life.

Susan's capacity to hold both grief and love while dying indicated a level of spiritual maturity, the capacity to accept *what is* with equanimity. Yes, she cried. Yes, she resisted. Yes, she said, "This is harder than I thought." And yet she always returned to her spiritual process of attuning to the mystery, and there she found comfort and support.

The Second Bookend is a rare glimpse into the process of completing a life in preparation for death. It is the full flowering of a life lived with love and courage, surrounded by family and friends and most of all, her beloved husband, Jorg. I'm tempted to say "a life too short," but the whole point of Susan's example is that this is a life just right.

Rachel Harris, PhD

Prologue

On good days, the sun is always shining. I have not opened my eyes, but I know it is sunny. I can feel the rays of the sun on my eyelids; the sunlight is making its way onto my face through a gap in the trees. This early in the day it is very quiet. I can hear the gentle flutter of wing feathers as a bird maneuvers its way onto the feeder that sits just outside of the screen, maybe six feet from the end of our bed. I am enveloped in the warmth from Susie; she is spooned against my back. I feel her regular and peaceful breathing. Life is good.

Then reality intrudes; she rolls out of bed and heads inside to pee. I hear the oxygen hose sliding across the floor. The flush of the toilet and then the cabinet door and the sound of pill bottles opening; time for the first two pills of the day, Nexium and Zofron. The morphine comes later. I hear an emphatic *No* as she once again informs the cat that attacking the oxygen hose is poor behavior. She is then back on the porch. I pull back the covers for her and she slides back into bed next to me. Her breathing is uneven from her short walk; I can feel little twitches in her skin where my arm is across her back. In a couple of minutes her breathing is back to what we now call normal. It is peaceful.

As I lie there with her head on my chest, and my arm around her shoulders, the sun on our faces, I say to her, "It looks like one more good day." She gives me a little squeeze.

Rob Jorgensen
August 2014

For Jorg

my best friend

my soul mate

my partner for over forty years

❧ · ☙

I cannot imagine a sadder, more tender parting, my Beloved.

PART ONE

This Side of Home

ONE

Seeds of Change

To us our house was not unsentient matter—it had a heart & a soul & eyes to see us with & approvals & solicitudes & deep sympathies; it was of us, & we were in its confidence, & lived in its grace & in the peace of its benediction. We never came home from an absence that its face did not light up & speak out its eloquent welcome—we could not enter it unmoved.

—Mark Twain[1]

1 from a letter to Joseph Twichell, published in *Mark Twain's Notebooks: Journals, Letters, Observations, Wit, Wisdom, and Doodles*, ed. Carlo De Vito (New York: Black Dog & Leventhal Publishers, 2015), 98.

Brushes with Death

I still find death amazing, don't you?
It seems so contrary to all of my assumptions.

—SCOTT TUROW[2]

May 1967   Author's close childhood friend dies at the
            age of sixteen in a car accident

March 1973 Marooned on the Rabbit Ears Pass
            (Steamboat Springs, Colorado) overnight
            under life-threatening conditions: 10,000
            feet elevation and temperatures near 0° F

July 1979   Author's beloved grandmother dies at the
            age of eighty-six

June 1989   Author's father slowly dies in hospital
            setting on a respirator fifteen days after
            failed heart bypass surgery

---

2 Lucy speaking to Seth following the funeral of his elderly father, from Scott
Turow, *The Laws of Our Fathers* (New York: Farrar, Straus and Giroux, 1996),
438.

January 1990   Author's mother dies in hospital setting of metastatic ovarian cancer three weeks after diagnosis

October 1992   Author's father-in-law dies in hospital setting of emphysema many years after diagnosis

November 1995   Author's mother-in-law dies at home, under the care of hospice, of metastatic breast cancer three years after initial diagnosis

April 2001   Author has revelatory dream of confirmation about love and wholeness

January 2004   Author's son is diagnosed with bipolar disorder

December 2005   Author diagnosed with Stage IIB, triple-negative primary breast cancer and she begins neoadjuvant chemotherapy

December 2005   Author's husband diagnosed with prostate cancer

February 2007   Author completes cancer treatment (simple mastectomy and reconstructive surgery)

May 2011   Author's husband struck by lightning and survives unscathed

June 2012   Family's nineteen-year-old cat dies at home of natural causes

May 2013   Author's thirty-four-year-old son commits suicide

October 2013   Author diagnosed with advanced primary adenocarcinoma with lepidic features in both lungs

I begin this book about death—what I have begun to call "the second bookend of life"—with a list of my own experiences around death and my close encounters with it. I have also included events that have helped me over time to expand the limited ways I had been dealing with it for most of my life. My family and I are no strangers to tragedy. But rather than drive us apart, as is often the case, our many adversities have served to draw us closer. Not that we didn't struggle mightily at times, and turn to blame and anger at others, because we did. But we always managed to find our way home to the love and comfort of each other's hearts. Instead of plunging us into despair, these experiences have become unexpected, valuable teachers. They have provided all of us with the opportunity to consider death in ways I never thought I would. Over many, many years, as I have pondered these events, my own perspectives and assumptions about death have changed dramatically. Between the ages of thirty-eight and sixty, I gradually learned that it was not only possible—it was actually helpful—to look at death within the context of *relationship*.

As I look back at the six-and-a-half-year period between 1989 and 1995, during which my parents and my husband's parents died, I sometimes lament, "If only I had known then what I know now..." My grief at times overwhelmed me and limited my vision to a common, myopic one in which death could only be a sadistic and cruel enemy. It simply was not possible in *my* universe that it could play any other role in my life. And I had learned somewhere along the line that it was simply wrong to talk about death. Wrong.

No one had ever suggested that having a relationship with death was even doable, let alone beneficial. At first, the newness of this framework seemed strange and uncomfortable, like a new pair of shoes feels until they're broken in. When that moment magically happens, the leather has softened, conforming to the lumps and bumps of each foot, and those stiff new shoes have mysteriously morphed into a second skin. Now my relationship with death has become those comfy shoes and it feels like one of the most natural things in the world. I experience it as healthy, helpful, useful, and valuable. I am aware that we have *so* much to learn about and from death.

What happens when we're unable to develop a relationship with death? Two emotions arise: fear and avoidance. All their cousins (denial, rejection, dread, panic, anxiety. . .) also begin to clamor for attention, and before you know it, our interior space is filled to overflowing with a fairly toxic soup.

As I began to tell people I was writing another book and they inevitably asked what it was about, I took a deep breath because the response was nearly the same universally. Most people knew that I had taken a week away—I called it my writing retreat—to concentrate on pulling together the many pieces that I'd been writing over the past seven years.

"So, how did your week go?" they'd ask innocently and with genuine interest. I could feel a familiar dread begin to rise up from my gut. I'd purposefully avoided making the focus of the book common knowledge: that dangerous, forbidden topic—death—had caused me to hesitate. Alas, I had more in common with my intended audience than I wanted to admit.

"It went really well. I couldn't believe how much I got done." My dread was beginning to look like a heavy fog overspreading a boggy marsh.

"What are you writing about?" This would be the next natural question and I would sigh to myself, "Oh, dear. Here it comes."

"Death. It's about death. I've actually been writing this book since I was going through treatment for breast cancer in 2006." By that point, I would find myself half holding my breath because *I* felt as awkward as I could see *they* did.

"Oh." This one-word response with a concluding period that was larger than a basketball was predictable and challenging for me.

No one knew where to go from that point—not them and not me—and I was the writer. Depending on the person and the situation, I'd either attempt to continue the conversation, or I'd change the topic, tossing off a comment like, "Kind of a conversation stopper, isn't it?" A short laugh would escape, brittle and forced, and we'd channel our chat into safer waters.

There appears to be a strong connection between this moratorium we've built around talking about death and our lack of an adequate language base that would help us have extended conversations about it. Another story comes to mind, this one around denial. A recent study was conducted with patients who'd been diagnosed with terminal lung cancer. All had chosen to pursue "palliative" chemotherapy and targeted treatments that would extend their lives by an average of two months. Their doctors had been clear that there was no cure for their cancers. When asked, however, 69 percent believed that their treatments would cure them.

This avoidance and denial aren't necessarily bad—they can help us get through the day. My therapist friend tells me the psychological term for this is "cognitive dissonance." Most of the time, my husband and I have been able to look death straight on and talk about it clearly. But there are some days when we just can't. We are fully conscious that we've chosen to live into the both/and of this: we can be brutally honest about our situation *and* we can't do it all the time. A typical conversation:

We're sitting on our porch at our round glass table with its white wicker base, the trees are shimmering their summer greenness in the sunlight, and we're probably looking at articles on the Internet or reading. The space between us is filled with peace and contentment. I remark, "Today's a good day." We try to say that to each other every day. Some days, my husband will chirp in, "And then there's the terminal cancer thing. . ."

"Oh, *that* again?" I will say, but my voice is light because I'm glad he's brought it up. Whatever it is that makes the levity possible, we're grateful and we inevitably roll our eyes at each other with a sort of *Oy, vey* expression and laugh. We've found a healthy way to dispel some of the trepidation and sorrow around my pending death. Some days, though, we simply can't approach the reality; it's too much, we're too tired, the day hasn't gone well—it could be any number of things that causes us to seek the fleeting relief denial provides. Because we can be so real with each other, I can look at the temporary denial and know how helpful it is to take a break from the harsh and unrelenting reality of my terminal cancer every now and then. However, as a long-term response, avoidance and denial aren't necessarily helpful in creating a stable, healthy foundation to help us deal with terminal illness and death.

Not long after I read that 69-percent statistic, I was working at my husband's office. The telephone rang and I answered perfunctorily, "Good day. Saren Engineering."

"Sue, is that you?" It was Judith, one of my husband's longtime business associates, and people always confuse me with the other woman who works with us.

"It is, Judith. Good to hear your voice; I haven't talked with you in a while." I responded warmly with my official business voice, which was already developing the hoarseness common to lung cancer patients.

"How are you?" she asked. Judith knew I had terminal lung cancer. I hesitated slightly, trying to decide how to respond honestly to her question. I didn't feel all that great that day but I also knew that I didn't need to go into details with her. Then I discovered that I didn't have to say anything at all because she'd begun to speak again without waiting to hear my answer.

"Is Rob around?" Even though her question about my health was sincere, she wasted no time getting to the point of the call.

"He is, but unfortunately he's on a conference call and I don't know how long it will take," I explained as I picked up my pen to take a message.

"Not to worry; it's nothing urgent. Just have him call me when he's finished. And I'm glad to hear that you're feeling well." Click. Call over, and I found myself momentarily stunned, staring at the phone. My puzzlement had knit my eyebrows together with an aching tightness. "Feeling well?" I had no idea that I felt well; facetiously, I thought to myself, "I'm glad she was able to let me know that." I knew she was sincere about wanting to know how I was feeling—and I also knew she wasn't able to go there with me.

When death becomes our focus, we tend to become alarmed, fearful, terrified, and anxious. It seems to me that this fear of dying and death colors everything from that point on. These potent emotions influence every decision we make around our medical care at the end of life, from our own care to the care of our loved ones. But how can decisions based primarily on fear and avoidance be in our best interest physically, emotionally, spiritually, and financially? These emotions support the invisible moratorium and our paucity of language about death.

All emotions have value and are important teachers. However, unconscious avoidance prevents honest conversation, and unchecked fear inflates an already dire situation; both block our ability to experience the full panorama of life. When avoidance and fear happen, our ability to make good decisions is compromised, so it's imperative that we look at what's happening and do what we can to mitigate any emotions that attempt to imprison us, inhibit us, render us incapable of fully participating in what's in front of us at this very moment.

I *know* it's counter-cultural to consider having a relationship with death and to perceive death as necessary and natural, an expression of completion and beauty. Because we live in a death-phobic society, there's little space to include this approach as *one* of the ways we relate to death. We're often desperate to stave off this inevitable moment. Our dis-ease has spawned billion-dollar industries that run the gamut from plastic surgery and expensive cosmetics to "palliative" chemotherapies that promise to extend our lives by those precious two months. "Perhaps those two months will give the researchers the time they need to come up with a cure," we think, we hope, we pray. We peck at these lines of comfort like hungry baby birds whose mother has just returned to the nest with our next meal.

What are some of the deeper issues that come up when we receive a diagnosis of a terminal illness? We're frequently devastated, stunned, thrown off balance. Our worlds are turned inside out and upside down before we even have time to draw our next breath. The unspoken words, "I don't want to die," tear viscerally and viciously at our hearts at odd times of the day and become an intrusive cacophony at night, rendering us restless, hovering at the edge of an abyss of despair. And alone. So alone. With whom can we share this silent, mute agony? With whom do we dare?

Companion concerns often sound like this:

What did I do to deserve this?

How will I ever tell my family?

Who's going to take care of my children?

I'm too young.

I have so much left to do before I die.

It's not fair.

Why is this happening to me?

I must have done something wrong to cause this illness or situation.

If only...

How could God let this happen to me?

How am I ever going to pay for my treatments?

How long will I be able to work?

Surely there is something we can do—you can do—that will help me live longer or maybe even cure me?

Most of the time, I suspect that "longer" actually translates at an unconscious level to "forever."

Most of these questions, unfortunately, have no satisfying answers, leaving us to scratch around the desert landscape looking for a vibrant underground spring with nothing more than a broken twig to help us out. The result: We filter out the valuable and essential questions about death, and we rush into action. If we can't answer these impossibly hard questions, we can at least treat the illness, even the ones with terminal prognoses, and feel like we are getting somewhere. We look for the paths that will restore some sense of power and control in the face of numbing loss and fear.

I have begun to call death the "second bookend" of life; the first of course is birth. I'm learning many things as I explore this bookend. It seems clear to me that most of us view death as completely separate from life. When we place death in this framework, we find ourselves literally at a dead end, with nowhere to go in any conversation. But to place death intimately *inside* life opens us up to limitless possibilities and an even deeper connection with life. It sounds counterintuitive, but over many years, I've learned that death isn't disconnected from life, but part of its essence. This new relationship that I believe is possible with death—the shift that I believe is beginning to happen at the margins of our culture—will help all of us expand and open our hearts to the completion and beauty that are as real and as present in our passing as are the tragedy and sorrow.

This new relationship reveals itself as a coin with two sides—the "both/and" phenomenon that continues to expand my own consciousness dramatically. And it's similar, if not identical, to the *vesica piscis* (*pisces* in some articles) drawings that predate all major religions of the current era. I'm finding great power in this tool as an effective way to blow apart our well-established patterns, attitudes, barriers, and limitations about death.

The sacred space of this configuration is referred to by many as the *mandorla,* an ancient symbol of two circles coming together, overlapping to form an almond shape in the middle. *Mandorla* is the Italian word for almond (see Chapter 5). The process of this overlap can open us up to discover—and to nurture—healthy, vibrant, helpful relationships with death. This is challenging, exciting, and incredibly hope-filled. My experience with mandorlas has helped me understand three things about them: they are always dynamic, they move in the direction of healing and wholeness, and they bridge two stances that appear to be in opposition.

This book is filled with stories; their ability to help us see things with new eyes is endlessly creative and surprising. Here's a small example: On the third day of my writing retreat—I'd taken the first day to rest and the second to consolidate all the haphazard pieces I'd been writing into one manuscript—I found myself discouraged that I'd be able to see this book to its end.

I e-mailed my mentor and muse that night, desperate and disheartened. "What am I thinking that I can pull a book like this off?" I wrote. Like a Mafia underling, I found myself muttering over and over, "Fuhgeddaboudit."

The next morning, I checked my email and there was her response. "Don't think about writing a book!!!" she advised. "Just essays, just chapters, just what you want. It will become a book because you're following your living process." What I heard her say was, "Tell your story." That was all I needed, and I began to write like I hadn't written in years; her sage advice had unleashed my pen. I began to see this daunting process of talking about death from the perspective of relationship and "both/and" as a series of stories whose wisdom about death would be revealed as the stories were told.

As a spiritual director, I've never ceased to be amazed by the power of our stories. All stories contain seeds of the sacred and can manifest the divine; that's part of their very nature. We come to know who we are by the stories that we tell. Our stories fashion us even as we fashion them. Each time we tell the story we may reveal something new, or we may hear it in a way we hadn't heard it before. This is the gift of story. Therapist Brian Jensen, in his article "Ancient Symbol of Wholeness," writes that "all good stories are mandorlas."[3] Some of the words he uses to describe the mandorla include healing, restorative, integrative, rebirth, and "a place of poetry...to remind us that there are links between the things we always thought of as opposites."

Stories seem to have a life of their own, connecting the seemingly disparate parts of our experience. Often, my directees (clients) would start telling me a story and then stop. "I think I've told you this story already," they'd say apologetically. "I don't want to repeat myself." Most of the time, I'd counter their hesitation with a quiet reply: "You may have—I'm not sure. However, I do know that, if you're moved to share this story now, there's some little kernel of wisdom or truth that wants to be discovered today." So they'd continue, and inevitably, an "aha" moment would catch both of us with surprise and delight. Some new insight would arise from the story that, even in the third or fourth telling, the storyteller hadn't seen or heard before simply because it hadn't yet been time for it to be revealed.

Each time I begin to tell or retell one of my stories focusing on death, two things inevitably happen: I learn something new, and/or the "thin space" to which the Celts often refer opens just a little more fully and clearly. Some refer to this place as the "other realm" or the "fourth dimension," frequented and beautifully described by mystics and poets. (I use all three terms interchangeably.) The stories that have come to me from this realm are by far the most moving, vivid, and revealing. From them, I have learned that death doesn't show up on our

---

3 Brian Jensen, "Mandala: Ancient Symbol of Wholeness," *Sandplay: The Sacred Journey* (Spring 1997).

doorstep naked or helpless, hungry or angry. Death brings its own teachers and guides to support us as we navigate this important life passage. Death does not abandon us. On the contrary, it confidently accompanies us across the final threshold as a faithful, trustworthy companion whose focus is our wellbeing and safety.

However, we must have eyes to see what is being shown and ears to hear what is being spoken in this realm. We must develop a curiosity and appreciation for the power of the sacred. How many of us, when asked, would or could answer "yes" if asked, "Are you curious about death?" Or if we were asked, "Do you appreciate death?" I imagine very few. Our fears and attitudes make it harder for us to seek, to receive, to welcome the guidance and support death offers each of us.

Not only have stories helped me learn how to be with death differently, the following quotes have also changed and expanded my awareness of death. They haven't taken away the pain, the loss, the tremendous grief that happens when a loved one dies, nor is that their goal. These words have been a gift and an oft-heard refrain in my head for many years now; each has taught me something important about this second bookend:

"Death be not proud, though some have called thee."[4]

These words have haunted and challenged me and ultimately taught me deep truths, even the viewpoints with which I have heartily disagreed; perhaps especially those because if they weren't resonating in my heart, then what was? Often, I felt like Jacob at the Jabbok ford (Genesis 32), wrestling many nights with these sensitive and oftentimes thorny issues. The conviction that there was some-

---

4 John Donne, *Holy Sonnets* (Newton, NJ: Vicarage Hill Press, 2014), 26.

thing important to discover here helped me stay the course. And it has been worth every minute. Each quote has revealed a particular wisdom that has helped me sort through my own story and experience with death.

John Donne's quote never made any sense to me; perhaps that's why I couldn't let go of it any more than it could let go of me. Over and over again I would hear it in my head, "Death be not proud." Whatever did that mean? Finally, I was able to respond with a modicum of clarity, "Death be not proud? Why not?" This response felt like a radical stance and yet one that reflects the truths I hold most deeply in my heart. I want to say, "Death, you are the complement for the birth bookend, you are its balance and its completion. You are natural and necessary to the cycle of life. You are beautiful."

I write this book from the perspective of a spiritual director and coach, my chosen profession for more than twenty-five years. Not familiar with the term "spiritual director"? My role is to help people connect with the sacred, divine, transformative, and life-giving experiences in their lives. The focus is on the spiritual *and* the religious, although many people consider themselves spiritual and not religious, or vice versa. People from all faith traditions and practices are welcome in my practice. From the outside, the process looks very much like therapy: I meet with folks one-on-one for about an hour once a month or so. What is required of both of us is deep, compassionate listening sustained by love in order to help my directees connect more deeply with the sacred. Being a woman and a spiritual director informs and transforms my every breath. They are two of the threads that weave the fabric of my being, anchoring the rest of the tapestry of who I am. Because of my perspective as a spiritual director, this is a book about God, by whatever name you use and whatever religion you follow, and about relationship with the living, the dying, and the divine.

TWO

Dying

"How did you learn how to die?" My friend asked me this question one day as we talked about the chemotherapy I'd received for my breast. She'd already wondered aloud what I'd do should my cancer metastasize or recur. I'd been undergoing tests for possible breast cancer in my other breast. I told her emphatically, "No more chemo. I'm not afraid to die." So how did I learn to die? I could only answer by telling her about one of the more important experiences of my life. This is that story.

It was the middle of March 1973. I'd be celebrating my twenty-second birthday in April; my husband had turned twenty-two the previous December. Two college friends, Dave and Eric, had come to visit us. Fresh out of college, just like us, they were making their way across the country from Connecticut to California in their van. I didn't realize that visiting meant living with us for a month in our rented eight-by-thirty-five-foot trailer. Lucky for me, I found out quickly that I enjoy the company of men!

"Everybody ready?" I'd called out to the lot of them. My anxiety had been building; it had taken us forever to get our gear, our clothes, and our daypacks ready for our biggest cross-country ski outing since we'd been living in Steamboat Springs, Colorado. We'd be making our way from the top of Rabbit Ears Pass to the top of Mount Werner—a bold plan that involved traveling more than ten miles over rough terrain, up a thousand feet of vertical gain, and through avalanche danger. At the age of twenty-two, anything and everything seemed possible.

By then, we'd lived through the assassinations of President John F. Kennedy and his brother Bobby, and of beloved civil rights leader Martin Luther King Jr. We were the first generation to watch a strange and difficult war unfold before our very eyes, live, straight from the battlefields into our living rooms. Into our brains, invited or not, like it or not, came the image of a naked child fleeing, face contorted in terror and pain, the village behind her engulfed in smoke and flames. These images had been indelibly etched. We were the generation who came of age as humans took their first steps on the moon.

By the time we'd reached young adulthood, we knew ourselves to be fragile in the face of senseless death and destruction. But we'd come through it all feeling invincible and passionate about making a difference, wanting to leave the world a better place. The early 1970s were an exciting time to be alive. We'd grown up in a time of transition: not only did all things *seem* possible; we *knew* them to be so. So that day in Colorado, the prospect of traversing ten miles of rugged terrain and a thousand vertical feet seemed eminently do-able—after all, we were living the fruits of our tumultuous history. We started the day full of confidence, excitement, and energy. Our love of being outside, in nature, skiing, propelled us forward, fired us up. We were, indeed, ready for anything.

This wasn't a round trip. We took off in two cars. Jorg and I followed Dave and Eric to the ski hill's parking lot so we could park our trusty '63 Chevy there. We piled into the back of Dave's van, and the four of us headed off for the pass. All of us, I think, were a bit concerned because we were starting later than we'd wanted to, but nobody said anything because, after all, we were invincible. By the time we'd waxed our skis, adjusted our daypacks, and decided the pecking order of skiers, it was a little after 11:00 in the morning and we were *finally* off.

We broke trail the whole way, most of the time bushwhacking, because in 1972, there just weren't that many cross-country ski trails around. This is hard on the leader because, even though it was March, it was still very much winter at ten thousand feet. At this elevation, spring wouldn't even begin to poke its curious little nose above the last vestiges of snow until two months later. The snow was deep and our skis sank with every step. Each time we thrust a ski forward, we could almost hear the muffled sound of the snow groaning, then thudding, as it gave way to our weight. The guys took turns as trail leaders; though I was a strident feminist, I was perfectly fine letting them break trail. Even feminists can take a vacation when it's convenient!

The day was stunning: a perfect late-winter day in the Rockies, with a high of 30 degrees, not a cloud in the sky, and no wind to speak of. Hard as it was on the trailbreaker, there were no adequate words to describe discovering meadow after pristine meadow without even the mark of an animal trail. The pounding of our hearts wasn't just from exertion; it was its own wordless response to the beauty, its own simple conversation.

Even though we were invincible, we weren't stupid, and we were also humble in the face of nature. We'd packed well, ready for all manner of exigency: we carried matches bagged in plastic, water, a ski tip or two, oranges, trail mix, a compass—just in case. You never knew. We realized we were just a speck in the presence of such fearsome wonder, chaos, and order. Despite our late start, we stopped periodically for water and snacks, followed by a longer stop for lunch.

Progress seemed agonizingly slow on this trip; time itself felt full of fatigue. That should have been our first warning sign that all was not well, but we chose to ignore it, blinded by our youthful vigor and enthusiasm. The drifts were huge in some places, and sinking in was taking a lot out of all of us. Mid-afternoon, I heard a crack and then an expletive. Eric was just in front of me. "Shit!"

"Eric, what's wrong?" He'd stopped in his tracks, and I skied up and planted my skis right beside his.

"My ski broke." Veteran downhill skiers, Dave and Eric had rented equipment just for this occasion. Jorg and I, on the other hand, considered ourselves accomplished cross-country skiers, and we'd been excited about showing them what fun it was. I'd begun to wonder by now whether Eric would agree; "fun" wasn't a word popping out of his mouth very often for the last hour or so.

We hollered up to Jorg and Dave, and they came back to where we were stopped. I wasn't worried because we had a plastic yellow ski tip, designed to slip onto a broken cross-county ski. We'd come prepared and our confidence remained unshakeable. Still. Eric's ski had broken clear in half, between the heel plate and the toe clip, and Jorg had to use the screwdriver on his Swiss Army knife to unscrew both pieces and move them to the front piece of Eric's ski. Progress was slow—his ungloved hands, chilled, chapped, and red, moved clumsily and took a while to attach the binding. In the end, Eric's ski was short but still better than nothing. Still, it made skiing more tedious, slower, and harder. The shadows were lengthening rapidly; winter afternoons seem to mysteriously gobble up the light. The guys had decided to take turns wearing the short ski to share the burden. I glanced at my watch: 3:00 pm.

Time for a pow-wow. I was the only one who'd begun to worry. I was the least experienced of all of us, physically the least conditioned, and the only woman, and I watched my invincibility ebb, my confidence waiver. And though I'd seen a man walk on the moon and belonged to the generation who could do anything, I'd begun to lose courage. I watched my own terror build as Eric struggled with his snapped-off ski in the middle of the Colorado Rockies, a million miles from anywhere. I knew, perhaps for the first time in my life, that we were less than the smallest specks in the middle of an unforgiving landscape of white, insignificant, uninteresting interlopers in the heart of a vast, heartless wilderness. We estimated that we were halfway from where we'd begun at the top of the pass to our destination at the top of Mount Werner. Somehow, turning back didn't seem to be an option, so we forged ahead.

Plus, we were circumventing a deep canyon. We knew this when we began our trek; it certainly wasn't news, but my overconfident husband hadn't been worried. Yet as we kept following the southern edge of this canyon, it seemed to have no end. This deep gouge in the landscape seemed determined to swallow us whole.

"So now what?" I asked. I heard my voice come out strained and thin, brittled by my nerves. I was scared. I was tired. I was mad at Jorg! We'd stopped yet again. We couldn't just keep following the canyon's edge further and further back into the endless wilderness. Our daylight would be gone in less than two hours.

"We're going to have to cross the canyon." Jorg's voice broke through nature's seemingly impenetrable silence, a knife's edge neatly dissecting our doom and divvying it up evenly among us. As much as I loved him and thought I knew him, I couldn't tell if he really was feeling brave or if he was pretending so as to quell my rising panic. It seemed to me we were all being remarkably calm considering the situation, but my inner raving madwoman was rapidly losing control and on the verge of escaping, and I was struggling to keep her in check.

Jorg continued thinking out loud, "I don't know how far back the canyon goes, and it's getting late. I had no idea it went back this far." We quietly began the arduous trek down into the canyon. It was too steep and treacherous to ski straight down, so we had to switchback, traversing the wall of the canyon, descending slowly and carefully. In the days and weeks and years that followed, I heard each one of the guys say how worried they were about avalanche danger. I am glad they didn't say it then.

It took about an hour to get across the canyon. The light was fading; all of us were tired. We left the canyon behind and came to a relatively flat spot where we would spend the night. Spend the night? Really?

Now, I'm a city girl. As much as I love the outdoors, I'd lived my whole life in a small house in a small city, where the hiking I did was on sidewalks and the only danger I knew was crossing the street without looking both ways and skinning my knees roller skating and playing hopscotch. I loved nature; I was raised in a family that loved nature—but nature meant picnics at a roadside table where the car—*the car*—was only ten steps away and *outhouses* were something other people used only under duress. No cars here. No outhouses within a hundred miles. Right about then, I was regretting every disparaging remark I'd ever made about them. At least they were some hallmark, crude as they were, of civilization.

"We're going to have to spend the night." None of us ever really said those words out loud; that would have made the situation far too real. Even so, those words hung heavily between us, sinking in slowly and suffocating us. My fear was palpable, tangible; it ran down my throat in rivulets and left a sour taste in my mouth. It had been a long time since our trailside lunch under the sparkling sun and the Colorado blue sky. No one else was saying much and I assumed I was the only one who was scared to death. I was going to die in the middle of the wilderness. No one was going to find my body. I was far too young to say it'd been a great life. I hadn't had even one of the children I knew I was destined to have. My bravery and self-confidence had vanished more quickly than kindling thrown on a hot fire.

These thoughts and fears—fortunately, I think—were conveniently crowded out by the immediacy of building a snow pit and gathering wood for a fire. We dug with our skis, we dug with our hands. We gathered wood as the thick, menacing gloom settled around us. As I watched these boy-men, I prayed that the fire would start before we ran out of matches. How did they know how to do all of this? Where did they learn? Jorg and Dave were clearly in charge, while I could sense Eric's unspoken fear. At that moment, we were more in tune with each other, more tortured by this situation. But there was no time to commiserate because all our energy had to be channeled into preparing for a long winter night in the middle of nowhere.

The fire caught before we ran out of matches. Relieved, we settled in for the night; the fresh pine boughs that lined the snow pit provided a bit of comfort. We were melting snow for drinking water in a plastic canteen—tricky at best, but eating snow was asking for trouble, as the energy it took for a human body to melt it was greater than the benefit of hydration. Sometimes, though, I snuck a handful because I was so thirsty. I felt guilty, like an alcoholic falling off the wagon.

We removed our skiing socks—more than thirty years later, I still have mine and Jorg's—and placed them to dry them by the fire . . . Norwegian snowflake socks, mine had big, green, vertical patterns running up the sides; Jorg's, less dramatic, had smaller snowflakes with a subtle magenta pattern. Scattered all over them are tiny brown marks where sparks flew from the fire and singed the wool. Whenever I take them out now, my finger reaches out to touch those marks; it's an instinctive motion that I can't control. I know on some level as I watch my finger that I'm watching an encounter with a near-death experience.

We slept in fits and starts. We told stories. We laughed. The story that elicited the biggest laugh was the one about the ski party that had gotten stuck out on this very pass just the weekend before. *They* had to be rescued. Ha, ha, ha! Look at us. *We're* not going to have to be rescued. Several members of their party were *still* in the hospital. More laughter. Ha. Ha. Ha. *We* were going to be fine. For me, it was false bravado; we weren't really making fun of them. Even as our hollow laughter rang, I was oddly comforted by our attempts at cheerleading. It helped us get through the night.

Finally, it was light enough to leave. We were grateful that the temperature hadn't plummeted. It was a "warm" night on the pass, somewhere around zero or so. We congratulated ourselves on our luck. Tired as we were, we appreciated a brand-new crystal clear, beautiful day, not a cloud in sight. To our relief and good fortune, no late winter storm was approaching. More bravado and blustering. Twenty-something guys are just so *good* at it! I was beginning to feel numb and oddly detached; it was almost like I was watching the scene unfold from a comfortable seat in the theater.

By noon, we were at the top of the ski hill. We'd traveled the eight miles; we'd been out for over twenty-four hours; we were still alive. We'd made it. Ta-da!

Had we? I wasn't so sure. Mount Werner was a popular ski area and now we were surrounded by throngs of downhill skiers swooshing down the mountain; it was the peak of the day. I'd never downhill skied. Not once. And here I was at the top of a very daunting ski hill—over three thousand vertical feet down and several miles to conquer. How would I ever do it?

We huddled again. Dave and Eric had been skiing the mountain every day during their visit, so they were familiar with the trails; they were also expert skiers. They decided to ski straight down—no easy task with cross-country skis, but they were confident. They were also tired and eager to be done with all of this. Jorg and I would stay together and he'd help me pick my way down.

I gave it the old college try. Standing at the top of this enormous mountain, watching people hop off the lift, looking down at what seemed to me a completely vertical cliff, there was no way I'd be able to do this. No way. My heart was pounding. Jorg was appropriately encouraging. I tried snowplowing. No luck. I couldn't get the edges of my skis to dig in. I tried zigzagging from side to side to minimize the vertical drop. I didn't care how long it took me; I just wanted to make it down the hill in one piece.

It must have been vacation week for every school system in the country. Suddenly, all these little people were skiing right by me. "Oh, look!" I heard one exclaim, "There's a cross-country skier! Let's see how close we can get!" Zoom! One flew by me so close I thought we'd end up in a death-delivering collision. I imagined us tumbling all the way down the hill, unrecognizable to anyone because we'd become a giant snowball with only our ski tips sticking out at odd angles. Finally, I couldn't be brave anymore. I skied gingerly down to the edge of the trail where Jorg was waiting patiently for me.

"I can't do this anymore. I really can't," I said with downcast eyes, feeling like I was letting him down. I was afraid he'd try to push me to ski further.

"So what do you want to do?" he asked.

"I don't know." I couldn't believe how tired I was. I didn't even know if I cared anymore. "No," I said emphatically to myself. "I have to care." We stood there for a few minutes in the warm afternoon sun, absentmindedly watching skier after skier fly past us with utmost precision and form. I'd become an elephant with only three legs, wearing roller skates instead of skis, and I was in a china shop. That's how graceful and competent I felt.

"OK." He'd come up with a plan. We decided to separate. I'd take off my skis and walk down the adjacent access road, designated as the rescue road for the ski hill. The snow there was packed hard and the ski patrol used it to transport the less fortunate skiers down on toboggans.

"I know exactly where the road comes out. I'll ski straight down, meet Dave and Eric, pick up our car, and meet you there." Sounded like a plan to me. We kissed as deeply as our dried-up and sunburned lips would allow. By then they felt more like singed parchment paper than human flesh; I half-expected to hear them crumple and then crack sharply. My fragile heart was breaking as I watched him turn and ski away. I could barely pick out his red parka by the time I started walking down the access road.

I watched numerous ski patrol guys come down the logging road, several with toboggans in tow. They said nothing to me. I said nothing to them. They didn't stop, and though I wished with all my heart that they would, I didn't call out and ask them to. I wasn't hurt, so how could I need them? I didn't scream; I didn't even whimper. I didn't wave my arms. I'd created this mess; it was my responsibility to get myself out of it.

I clearly remember saying this to myself: "I don't need them. I'm walking down the mountain on my own two feet, under my own power. No broken bones. My skis are perched on my left shoulder. Why would I stop them?" What *was* I thinking? The simple answer was that I *wasn't* thinking. The wisdom of many years has taught me that there's a fine line between being stubborn and stupid. I'd just crossed the line to "stupid."

The going was slow. One foot up. One foot down. Up and down my feet went; I felt like I was participating in a vivid nightmare. Sometimes I was able to establish a rhythm, sometimes not because my cross-country ski boots had an awkward square toe where they attached to the ski. Hard to walk in. Sometimes it was just hard because I sank a bit in snow softened by the warmth of the afternoon.

Finally, I neared the bottom of the mountain. The sun was low in the March sky and naked tree limbs cast long, bony fingers across the logging road. They seemed accusatory and cruel. The snow looked cold and uninviting after thirty hours in the wilderness without adequate food and drink. Everything seemed threatening, dark, and dangerous now. I was so tired I could barely believe that I could still pick one foot up and set it down and then do the same with the other.

I stumbled. I fell. I was sprawled out in the snow, face down, a reverse snow angel. My yellow down parka and my dark green, snow-flaked singed ski socks stood out in bright relief against the pristine white landscape. I realized that I was looking down, seeing myself lying there even as I was still in my body; somehow my consciousness had split in two. I was acutely aware of how good the cold snow felt on my sunburned face. I laid there reveling in the immediate relief it brought. I'd stopped worrying. I was too tired even for that.

I closed my eyes. Suddenly I knew beyond a shadow of a doubt that death was here. The Grim Reaper had his scythe swinging rhythmically and he was ready. *I really was going to die here, at the bottom of this mountain.* Nature would have its way. Gone was the panic of the day before when the same thought surfaced as we built the snow pit. Gone was the paralyzing fear. In its place, I was flooded with peace. Not just a wish for peace. Not just a fleeting moment of peace. A peace that had infused itself into every molecule of my being. It felt supernatural.

A quiet like I'd never known before blanketed my being. I "heard" words, not from a voice inside or outside my head but emerging from the birth canal of the universe. They were so substantial that they became a tangible presence. "It's OK." I rested in these words. I had done everything I could do. I had no energy to get up. No energy to make a sound. And I knew, as I'd never known anything before or since, that I was OK. I was far more than OK. I was excellent. I was without fear. I was immersed in, surrounded by, infused with the deep peace of the universe. How could I not be OK?

Of course, that wasn't the end of the story. You know that, because I've lived to tell it. What came next remains, to this day, a mystery. Such a mystery that I don't know what comes next. In that moment and in the moments that followed, I lost time. I simply don't remember getting up; I don't remember anyone helping me get up. Time folded in upon itself like an old blanket and a part of my story is hidden in that crease. It's like someone tore a page out of an adventure novel. It's just gone and its absence isn't at all satisfying.

The next scene I remember is this one. I was walking to the car. Jorg was holding the passenger side door open for me, a can of cold soda in his hand. I imagine that he was grinning broadly although I can't remember that for sure; I definitely remember the soda. I grabbed it from him. I wanted to guzzle it down in one gulp but I couldn't because I was dehydrated—I hadn't known that dehydration causes your throat to swell and severe dehydration makes it impossible to swallow even one small drop. That was why the party that was rescued the previous weekend had to be hospitalized—they all needed intravenous hydration and treatment for exposure.

I could only manage to swallow drops. *Drops.* Hardly enough. My aching raw throat couldn't manage any more than this one small, stingy, grudging drop at a time. At this rate, I gauged that my twelve-ounce can of soda would take a week to consume. I was struck by the irony of being too thirsty to quench my own thirst adequately. I don't remember if I kissed Jorg or not. My brain was on overload. I handed my skis to him, I numbly slid into the passenger seat and closed my eyes. The words came out one at a time, and I sampled each one as if it were a rare delicacy, digesting slowly, savoring in amazement. I. Am. Alive.

Years ago, I attended a meeting of a board of directors and, as is often the practice, we began our day with an exercise commonly referred to as an "ice breaker." The question we were to consider was, "What experience has been one of the most life-changing for you?" This is the one that I return to time and again. It continues to frame everything that's followed it. And it also seems to be always happening in the "*now.*" Everything has unfolded within this framework. The voice of the universe that spoke so fiercely to me, "It's OK," was timeless, not linear; it is speaking to me *now*, even as I type these words. It arises from the mysterious other realm and returns there. I hear it today as I heard it then. I know the truth of it today as I knew the truth of it then. I feel it in every bone, every muscle, every fiber, and every molecule of my being. It comforts me now as much as it comforted me then.

"It's OK" is the phrase I hear. Another quotation has also helped me. It was eloquently penned by the fourteenth-century English mystic and anchoress, Julian of Norwich. She wrote it in an essay that's recognized as the earliest surviving book written in the English language by a woman, *Revelations of Divine Love*, also known as *The Shewings*. "All shall be well," she wrote, "and all shall be well and all manner of thing shall be well." We can't, as human beings, see the full picture or come to absolute understanding of her wisdom and revelation; it is not part of our nature to do so. We can, however, experience the grace of acceptance, as she did.[5]

I'd been speaking to a friend recently about the peace I'd felt after falling on that fateful March day at the bottom of Mount Werner. For some reason, we'd also been talking about my mother and her death in the same conversation. Suddenly, a connection was made that I hadn't been aware of. I didn't feel that *I* had made the connection—it just appeared, as things from this other realm are wont to do.

My mother died of metastatic ovarian cancer. Oddly enough, that was the last diagnosis she ever expected to receive because she'd thought her hysterectomy in 1966 had removed both her ovaries. Exploratory surgery on Christmas Eve 1989, though, revealed that her doctor had left one ovary in place, a cruel twist of fate.

After spending nearly two weeks in the hospital, she was miserable. The surgery was the icing on the cake, revealing so much cancer in her peritoneal cavity that the surgeon couldn't see most of her organs. The aggressive cancer had become like glue, binding everything into one toxic mass. The specialists gave her two options: a radical chemotherapy intravenous drip that would take twenty-four hours or transfer to another hospital an hour away for radical surgery to remove as much of the cancer as possible.

---

5 *Revelations of Divine Love*, which also bears the title *A Revelation of Love—in Sixteen Shewings* (Norwich, England, 1395), Chapter XXVII.

My mother chose the drip, the strongest chemo cocktail available at the time. Two days after the infusion, she suffered a pulmonary embolism in the early hours of the morning, giving her, at most, only a few days to live. Standing in her hospital room the day she died, tenderly hugging her, I was told by the doctor that this particular blend of chemicals either cured you or killed you.

I'd just driven home to Connecticut from my mother's home in central New York when I got the news of her embolism. I remember my hands were trembling even more than my heart as I threw random clothes in my suitcase, including my "Sunday best," because I knew I wouldn't be home again until after her funeral . . . until she was—oh, unthinkable thought—dead. In went my dress boots, in went my best winter dress, and over my arm I carried my heavy, long wool winter coat. I couldn't bear the thought that persistently repeated itself over and over, a dreary, off-key, poorly written, pre-funeral dirge: "Your mother will be dead when you wear these things."

I'm not sure there are words to describe the strangeness of that, to know beyond a shadow of doubt that I was acting in light of an unimaginable tragedy that had yet to happen. It was in this frame of mind that I turned around, retraced my steps, and made the four-hour trip back on the New York State Thruway. I was in a state of anxiety, praying like crazy, doing my best breathing to help me focus as I drove in the midst of heavy snow that created near white-out conditions on parts of the road. The Albany–Utica leg of the thruway is one of most desolate, empty patches of road I've ever driven. It seemed to match and then magnify my own mood.

By the time I reached the hospital, the light had long since given way to the darkness that only winter nights seem to possess: thick and nearly impenetrable, a true barrier to all that feels life-giving. I went to my mother's bedside, drew up a chair, and held her hand. She'd had a DNR order put on her chart, and it seemed that this was the one thing that weighed most heavy on her mind and heart.

"I've had a DNR put on my chart," she said haltingly. She paused, whether to wait for her limited breath to return or simply to find the courage to go on, I didn't know.

"I hope I've done the right thing." Her hair made a soft whispering sound as she rotated her head on the crisp hospital linens in order to make eye contact with me. Her pale blue eyes seemed to contract into a space my own could not access. I was here and she had fallen into some unfamiliar space that had room for only one.

"Oh, Ma, of course you have. Who would expect you to continue to endure all this for any longer than you have to?" But my words didn't sound all that convincing to me and I'm sure they sounded equally hollow to her. Even though I supported her decision 100 percent, I felt unskilled and inexperienced around this topic. I knew that no amount of my conviction could suddenly migrate from my heart into hers. I found myself absurdly full of regret that there was no mechanism to transfuse emotions from one person to another as easily as there was for blood.

Our conversation was short lived. I was as tired as she was. Two days later, I drove back to the hospital to keep vigil with her. I'd tried to stop at a local church to simply sit, pray, absorb the holy; my plan was stymied because the priest was in the midst of preparing for a Saturday morning wedding. I sighed, left, and got in my car for the two remaining miles to the hospital. When I got there, I thought I'd stop at the coffee shop, but "something" was urging me to "go to your mother's room and stop dawdling around."

Walking into her room, the first thing I noticed was that the oxygen that was helping her to breathe had a steady sound to it. There was no sense of any activity, which seemed strange and out of place. It was about 9:30 and the nurses had finished their morning rounds. My mom was comfortably propped up on pillows that had been expertly plumped and carefully arranged. Her bedding was smoothly and lovingly drawn around her and her arms were resting comfortably by her sides; her hands were relaxed. There was no perfunctory attitude here about each patient's morning routines and rituals. The nurses had taken good care of her—not a hair on her head was out of place and she looked wonderful.

However, in one of the biggest "aha" moments I've ever had, I knew instantaneously that she was dead. I blinked. I swallowed hard. I'd found my mother dead in her hospital bed. I didn't have a script for this one and it certainly wasn't like *this* in any movie I'd ever seen. The only thing I knew with complete certainty was that I couldn't leave her. She was still warm, so she hadn't been dead that long. I dragged a heavy metal chair with a faux-leather green seat to the side of her bed and sat down; the vinyl was sticky, the padding hard as stone; it squeaked a half-hearted protest when I lowered myself onto it.

I took her hand in mine and just held it. I wasn't having profound thought or insight; I think I was numb and trying to keep my wits about me. Plus, I was overwhelmed with how wrong it would have felt to leave her. And so I waited. I was sure someone would come soon. Wouldn't they? They had to, didn't they? One minute inched and crawled agonizingly into the one ahead of it, a slow column of ants that had been drugged senseless. I wasn't sure there was any grace to be had in this moment.

My brain was empty. My heart was a hard, lumpy rock inside my chest cavity; it felt like it had stopped beating. As the landscape of the hospital room began to take on a more and more surreal air, like a Salvador Dali painting, I began to wonder if perhaps I was dead, too. At any moment, I was sure a bleached and barren skull would appear on the floor in front of me.

Agitation began to replace my initial numbness. At least I was feeling something. Thirty long minutes passed, or rather dragged piteously along. Time became an old workhorse nearly unable to pull his rusted-out plow one furrow farther. I'd never known one minute could last this long, let alone thirty of them; each contained a complete lifetime of agony all by itself. A strange version of hell had opened its doors wide, pulled me in, and wasn't going to let me out.

Finally, I *had* to do something. I managed to let go of my mom's hand. I managed to stand up. I managed to move my legs. Ah! Relief. I could walk. I wasn't dead and it wasn't a nightmare. I could walk straight out of Dali's painting. I reached the door to her room and stepped into the hall. I didn't have a plan. I felt like, were I to look into a mirror, my eyes would be hollow and empty all the way back into the hell I'd just left. I wasn't sure where my soul was.

Immediately outside the door of her room, there was a service elevator. Waiting there was a nurse and an elderly man on a gurney. I assumed she was bringing him somewhere for some procedure. I opened my mouth. I didn't know what I was going to say, but what came out shocked me, "Where in the *hell* are all the nurses? My mother is dead in her bed!" Even then, I knew this was the sort of black humor one might find in a Mel Brooks or Monty Python movie. Only this wasn't a movie; this was my life. And my mother was dead.

The poor nurse looked stunned. She stuttered. "You'll . . . you'll . . . you'll have to go to the front desk. I have to take my patient down to x-ray right now." Mercifully, the elevator doors opened, she moved the gurney inside, the doors closed, and I was left standing there alone, my mother fifty feet away across the miles and miles of unnavigable space I could not travel with her.

I made it to the nurses' station and things began to happen as one expects them to happen when someone dies. Doctors and nurses appeared. The mortician was called. We'd finally found the lost script and could proceed as protocol dictated. I could breathe again and the shock of it all began to subside. The relief was palpable. I've often wondered what that patient must have thought as I sputtered those words out, "My mother is dead in her bed." I'm not sure what I would've thought if I'd been him. Mostly, I just put the experience into the drawer labeled "macabre" and left it there.

It took me many years to come to terms with that experience. There were times when I knew I'd dissociated because the event was simply too hard, unexpected, and foreign to take it in all at once. But when I was talking to my friend recently about it, I was surprised that what I was most aware of was the peace in her hospital room when I walked in. I'd missed that the first time around. In all the countless times I'd gone back over those awful moments, I'd failed to notice it. I could've rationally told you that she died peacefully because she looked peaceful. There wasn't one wrinkle in her bedding, she was sitting up, there was no telltale evidence of thrashing about or fighting some ferocious, invisible enemy who'd come to capture her. The visual evidence of a peaceful passing was too strong to think otherwise. I found welcome comfort in that. However, I'd never *felt* it until that conversation with my friend.

Suddenly, I *knew* the peace. I *felt* the peace. I *recognized* the peace. I remembered a Bible passage that is one of my favorites:

And the peace of God, which surpasses all understanding,
will guard your hearts and your minds in Christ Jesus.

—Phillippians 4:7 (New Revised Standard Version)

And then I realized that the peace that surrounded my mother as she was making her way through the death passage was one and the same peace I'd felt that cold March day in Colorado when I was convinced I was dying. With this new awareness, I began to wonder about my absolutely unnerving, unshakable conviction that I couldn't leave her bedside. I felt like the subject of the Rolling Stones' song, "Wild horses couldn't drag me away." I began to ponder that she'd been in the middle of some part of the dying process and I needed to remain until that part was complete. I'll never know the answer, but it makes sense to me, it "fits," it feels congruent. I believe that this "peace that surpasses all comprehension" is part of the beauty of the death experience. I've known it, I've felt it, I've recognized it with others. It's as personal and intimate as it is universal.

THREE

Dead

"We will all die," writes poet Naomi Shihab Nye in *Words Under the Words*.[6] This was never truer for me than when my dad passed away. The particulars of his death changed me forever, changed my relationship with the medical system, changed my own thoughts about how I wanted to die should I ever be confronted with a long-term terminal illness. I doubt that I'd have been compelled to write this book had it not been for my father's death.

This story's roots began in June 1969, when my dad had his first heart attack—no warning signs, just boom! Walking and talking and then in the ICU actively engaging with his first struggle with death. He survived, changed his lifestyle—less eating, no more smoking, more regular exercise. He set up a rowing machine in the basement of my childhood home. He worked diligently to maintain his health . . . and he was successful until June 1987. It had been a good eighteen years. From the outside looking in, he seemed to integrate the restrictions his heart disease placed on him with little fanfare. He was my unqualified hero and I was in awe of how he made the adjustments he needed to and never seemed to complain.

---

6 Naomi Shihab Nye, *Words Under the Words: Selected Poems* (Portland, OR: Far Corner Books 1995).

In 1987, my father, known to almost everyone as Dick, was sixty-four years old. He was a barrel-chested man about six feet tall and he wore horn-rimmed glasses—had as long as I could remember. His short, salt and pepper hair was getting thin on top, something I teased him about all the time. Our relationship was warm and cordial, despite his tendency to be close-lipped and stingy with his words and feelings. He was a World War II veteran, a Navy man, went to college after the war on the GI Bill. The summer after he graduated in 1949, he was a golf pro at a state park in New York. He met my mother when she came for golf lessons. She'd been a lieutenant in the Navy Nurse Corps—a beautiful woman with soft, wavy brown hair and a figure most women only dreamed of. I never once saw her hold a golf club. I've always found it funny that I'm here because someone invented a little white ball that people liked to hit with strange-looking clubs.

Like many veterans, my dad didn't talk much about the war; instead, he'd take out a tattered black and white snapshot of him in his everyday uniform, sitting on a lower bunk in the sleeping area. Many times, he told me the story of all the guys on the ship, bored one day, giving each other Mohawk haircuts. Mohawks? Really? I knew every line of this story by heart. In the photo, they all looked pretty funny; they had an alien look about them that scared me a little when I was younger. He'd laugh; I'd laugh; this precious memory still makes my heart dance every time I think of it.

He'd also talk about almost marrying an English girl he'd met on leave during the war; she lived in London and her name was Beryl Clatworthy. My mom would tease me when the story would come up, gesturing with her thumb and forefinger nearly touching, that I came "this close to being an Englishwoman and having Beryl Clatworthy for a mother." Those were the only stories he'd ever tell me about that time in his own young life; he was twenty-two when the war ended. It was only later, as I became an adult, when I realized how truncated his war stories were—how much was missing, how much he couldn't share because it was just too painful. The sixtieth anniversary of D-Day touched me deeply; by then, my dad had been dead for twenty-five years. He'd been on the boats that had carried so many GIs to their deaths. Where did you store the horror of those days, Dad? My own heart searched for a reflection of his soul in the eyes of the few living men who shared their memories with TV interviewers.

This was my dad. In 1987, he drove himself to the emergency room because his angina had become too much; he was afraid he was having a second heart attack. While on the examining table, he went into cardiac arrest. They shocked him back to life. Everyone who worked on him as he was lying on that table said over and over again that it was a miracle he survived. Had he been at home, had he been in his car, had he been, in fact, anywhere but lying on the examining table in the local emergency room, he would have died. Dead. That's it. His heart had stopped completely.

Because I lived four hours away from my parents, I didn't arrive until a long, wrenching day after my mom called to give me the news. My dad was in his hospital bed by now. My mom was naturally distraught and shaken, couldn't talk about it very much. Terror had rendered her normally sallow complexion a disconcerting shade of white. When my dad and I were finally alone, he lifted his undershirt and showed me his battle wounds—four bright red, distinctive rectangles that were caused by the clappers. My eyes opened wide in shock and disbelief. We were light-hearted though, giddy almost. We were glad to be able to share at this level; these were wounds he *could* talk about.

We weren't ignoring the enormity of what had happened. We were just more relieved that he was here and I was here. I could squeeze his hand and he could squeeze back, warm and vibrant flesh pressing into equally warm and vibrant flesh. I could kiss his whiskery cheek. I could exclaim, "My dad's alive." The words became a joyful dancer pirouetting elegantly in my head. I could feel grateful that my mom, my brother, and I weren't planning his funeral right this minute. Cold shudders ran through me as I reflected on how close we'd come to that scenario.

I asked him, part playfully, part out of curiosity, part out of a desire to let him talk about the experience, "So Dad, did you have a near-death experience? Did you see the white light, did you walk down a tunnel— you know, all the things people talk about when they almost die?" My curiosity was burrowing a huge nest in my head.

He shook his head; I could hear his short, coarse hair rub against the stiff hospital pillowcase. "No."

"No? Aw, cm'on. What do you mean, no? All that drama, all that opportunity, and nothing?"

"Nothing. All I remember is lying on the table, looking up at the bright ceiling lights. Next thing I know, I open my eyes and see a whole bunch of people huddled around me. That's it."

"Bummer," I said, oddly disappointed. "At the very least, after all this, you could've come out with a near-death experience, don't 'cha think?"

"Yeah," he agreed. We were half-laughing at the absurdity of all of it—of his close encounter, of this conversation, of life, of death, of everything.

"OK." I wanted this light-hearted bantering with this man I loved so much to continue for as long as it could. Truly. I wanted it to go on forever. My eyes narrowed a bit as I looked into his. "No trying this again just to see if you can have one. OK?"

"Yeah, no kidding." He agreed, nodding his head in assent this time.

Then I turned serious. There *was* something important that I wanted to say to him, in this place, in the absence of my mom, who was too scared to talk about any of this. I was a little nervous about my request; I'd never asked anyone to do something like this. Ever. I took a deep breath to steady myself, to stall for time, to find the courage.

"Dad?"

"Yeah?"

"There's something I want to ask you. . . ." I hesitated as I searched for the next words. "A favor." Seemed like a silly thing to say—there he was, laying in a hospital bed just recovering from a massive cardiac arrest and there I was, an able-bodied young woman capable of leaping tall buildings when put to the test. And *I* was asking *him* to do *me* a favor. I was at a loss as to know how better to start this conversation.

I took another deep breath. "Dad. You know, when you really do die . . . ." My voice trailed off and stopped. What was I saying? I couldn't believe I was actually able to get these words out of my mouth. No one talked about death and dying like this. I must have been crazy.

"Yeah."

"Well. I don't want to get a phone call telling me that you're dead. You know?"

"Yeah." Like I said, he was a man of few words. But he was listening intently; I knew this because we were making lots of eye contact.

I took another deep breath and continued. "I want you to be able to let me know, you know, um, when you're on your way up to heaven. I think you'll be able to give me a sign or something." Phew. Finally this bizarre request was actually out of my mouth. "You know what I mean?" I was desperate for some response from this man who was my father, some response that assured me, some response that told me that he got this crazy thing I was asking him for. It was selfish, I knew, and yet I also think it was good for both of us to be able to say these things to each other. None of us lives forever and we were learning together how to talk about It. We were actually having an honest conversation about death.

"Yeah. Like a tap on the shoulder?" He suggested this.

"Yeah. Like a tap on the shoulder." The conversation was over. We didn't talk about it again, not once, until two years later.

By then my dad's heart wasn't getting stronger. His meds were maxed out. There was nothing more the doctors could do for his crippling angina except quadruple bypass surgery. The city my mom and dad lived in had no hospital that routinely performed this procedure, so they traveled by ambulance to a hospital three and a half hours away. My mom, brother, and I were staying in a former nursing school dorm that had been converted to housing for the families of patients.

The trip to this hospital was a five-and-a-half-hour drive for me. I arrived the day of the surgery, after my brother, and I found all of them—my mom, my dad, and my brother—in a little cubicle in the prep area. My dad was sitting up in bed; his IV had already been inserted into his right hand. My mom and my brother were standing together, on his left side. I went over and stood on his right side. None of us had much to say. Waiting for the surgical nurses to take him into the operating room was an awkward time. We were all afraid, I think, and didn't know how to talk about that or about what was really on our minds. Would my dad live? Or would he die? Thoughts too big to think, never mind give voice to.

At one point my dad looked over at me and made eye contact. I looked back into his blue eyes with a steady gaze. He said one brief thing. "Remember, tap on shoulder." I didn't know if I heard it as a question or a statement; it didn't matter. I blinked a few times rapidly to keep the tears from coming. I could only nod my head as I thought, "This is it. He's just told me that he's going to die." It was a brief exchange, although not one lost to my mom and my brother.

The nurses came. They took him away. He was brave. We were brave. Four brave people contemplating death without knowing how to say one word about it. However, my mom and my brother pounced on me as soon as he was gone. "What did he mean, 'Tap on shoulder'? What did he mean?" Their tone was insistent and felt invasive. I shook my head and mumbled something incoherent. I felt shy talking about death. I also felt that I couldn't share this intimate moment my dad and I had had without somehow violating its sacredness.

We all went into the cardiac waiting room. The hours piled up. One. Two. Three. Four. They felt like lead bricks in my heart until I was certain that my very foundation would cave in under the weight of them. Still we heard nothing. I was mending the bottom of a sweater; at least when I had the elastic thread and needle in my hands, I was not painfully picking at my cuticles. Families came and families went, a parade of hopeful faces full of visible relief. The loved ones they had been waiting for had come out of surgery and were resting comfortably. They rushed to hold hands and exchange tender kisses. I began to think we were stuck in a *Twilight Zone* time warp specially crafted just for us.

Finally, one of the operating room nurses came down and told us that my dad was in recovery. It had been a difficult surgery; it had been hard to find enough healthy parts of his heart to do the grafts.

More time passed. We went to the bathroom even though we had no urge. We drank coffee and soda even though we weren't thirsty. We mindlessly flipped pages of books we couldn't have cared less about. My mom fidgeted, picked at her ragged cuticles, just like I was doing, and sighed a lot. In that moment, as different as we were, we were mirror images of each other. Periodically, the hospital intercom harped at our ears, dispassionately shattering whatever quiet we might have found. The waiting was carving great bloody underwater caverns in our hearts. There was no escaping this ocean of agony.

Suddenly, miraculously awakened from my waiting room stupor, I heard actual words over the intercom. It was a Code 4 in the recovery room. The urgent warning bounced around the waiting room walls like a ping-pong ball. I wanted to duck and cover my ears to hold back the sound. I knew it was my father. I felt my energy shift. He was dying. I could feel his spirit slipping away. Tears began to roll slowly, silently down my cheeks. I hoped my mom didn't see me; I didn't want to tell her what I knew.

And then the shift stopped. I lost the feeling completely and didn't know what was happening.

The nurse came down again and told us that they'd taken my dad back into the operating room because he'd gone into cardiac failure. A new round of hand wringing ensued. Three hours later, the nurse reappeared and told us that they'd stabilized him by inserting a heart pump into the artery from his leg. The pump would keep the artery open so that his heart didn't have to work so hard.

My dad never left the Cardiac Intensive Care Unit; he "lived" there for fifteen days. Our days were filled with conferences with doctors; I found solace and comfort in long walks along the tree-lined residential streets of the city. I cut out my older daughter's sixth grade graduation dress on the floor of the nursing dorm lounge; it was light blue cotton dyed so that it looked like eyelet. My brother and I shared a dorm room. My mom seemed to adjust to dorm life and cafeteria food far better than we did. I learned quickly to whine about everything.

Each day, my dad grew a little weaker. Strong medications, the heart pump, and the respirator were keeping him alive. I was not impressed that medical technology had made it impossible for him to die. The doctors had put him on medications that immobilized every muscle and shunted all his blood to his major organs. His incisions had become necrotic and his toes had lost their pink color and were turning a blue-black shade. My dad was a tall man, and his poor dying toes peeked out at me from the bottom of the white hospital sheets every time I walked into his tiny cubicle. I couldn't ignore them. "We're dying, too," they seemed to say. They seemed to want me to hear their part of the story of this horrible death and become their advocate in some way.

I caught one of his medical team in the hallway one day. I said, "My father's toes are turning black."

He replied, "Mrs. Jorgensen, that is the least of our problems right now. We are trying to stabilize him while his heart heals."

"But what about quality of life? My dad loves to golf and garden. He wouldn't want to live if you have to amputate his feet."

"We are doing the best we can. He still has about a twenty percent chance of surviving." Twenty percent? I was incredulous. I didn't know what else to say because the absurdity of his comment had rendered any response meaningless. Twenty percent? Our conversation ended abruptly.

After about twelve days, my mom and my brother had to stop going in to see him. His condition had so deteriorated that visits were too upsetting. We didn't know if he could hear us; he couldn't respond because the medications had paralyzed his muscles. I continued to go to his cubicle. Right about then, I sensed a shift in my dad. Part of it was that his wounds had begun to smell. Was this the smell of death, I wondered? I mentioned it to the nurse. She was grateful. She said, "We rely on the information from our patients' family members. They are much more aware than we ever could be." Her comment made me feel somewhat useful in the midst of days and days of feeling completely useless.

I would keep my dad informed about the weather, the food, what I had seen on my walk that day—stupid stuff, anything to fill the time. Many times I silently lamented that I was not a natural-born comedienne. Why couldn't I channel the spirit of Lily Tomlin when I most desperately needed her? I resorted to holding his hand and telling him often that we loved him. I felt so inadequate. Each time I left his cubicle, I contorted myself, a regular human Gumby, to carefully circumvent the tangle of tubes so that I could kiss him on the forehead.

His kidneys began to fail. His internists called in a nephrologist to consult about dialysis. This doctor was an older man, heavyset and olive-skinned, with deep black eyes beneath thick eyebrows. His soft, well-worn, wool sports coat added to the gentleness of his demeanor, and I immediately warmed to him. There was no real consultation room adjacent to the cardiac ICU, so, after he finished examining my dad and reading his chart, he took us into what looked like a supply area for some semblance of privacy.

He shook his head sadly as we each awkwardly found a place to stand in this tiny space. He told us in heavily accented English, "I will not put your father on dialysis. He is in God's hands now."

My mom crumbled. I put my arm around her. There wasn't much more to say. We thanked him and watched him walk down the empty hallway; the waning sound of his footsteps became a muffled echo that bounced around the chambers of my heart: my dad is dying, my dad is dying. More slowly now . . . my . . . dad . . . is . . . dying. At the same time, the doctor's gentle honesty felt like a savory balm, something we had not encountered often in the sterile hospital landscape. To this day, I can still see those dark, dark eyes fill with compassion and I can still feel the energy of his kindness wrap around the three of us.

I was relieved. Perhaps this long nightmare would be over soon. Like a slow jogger, remnants of guilt lapped around my internal conversations because I was afraid it was wrong to want my dad to die. What normal, decent human being feels that way? Yet I knew that none of us—my dad included—could suffer like this for much longer. No matter how hard I prayed and how much I wrote in my journal, I was unable to find any meaning that made sense to me or provided any morsel of comfort.

Just after that, my mother pleaded with me tearfully, "I just want to hold him one time without all those stupid tubes and machines. Just once."

"I know, Ma, I know." I patted her hand, I hugged her. I didn't know what else to say and I didn't know what avenues to pursue to change any of this.

The day before he died, I talked again with the internists. Always, it seemed, these conversations took place as we were walking down a hospital hallway. "You have to take my father off the respirator. Otherwise, I am going to be burying two parents; my mother can't take much more of this."

"Well, Mrs. Jorgensen," the doctor's tone was crisp and official sounding, "we will need to call a meeting of the board to review his case and get their permission first. There will be papers to sign, of course, by his next of kin." This was my dad he was talking about, not some corporate merger. How could he be so detached?

"How soon can this happen?" I pressed him, undeterred by his officiousness.

"Well," he paused, calculating the process in his head. "Not any earlier than tomorrow."

"I don't care what you have to do. We'll sign whatever needs to be signed. There will not be a problem there, I can assure you." My voice was tight and very controlled. It was all I could do to refrain from shaking him.

"All my mother wants to do is hold my father in her arms one time without the respirator in the way. That's all she wants." I held my voice steady and firm. I was nearing wits' end and the tears were close to the surface. I was determined not to let this doctor witness my distress. I didn't know why I felt guilty and I couldn't explain why I felt a little like the hooded executioner holding the bloodied axe in my hand. Again, the question asserted itself with a startling insistence: Was it wrong to want my father to die, and sooner rather than later? Was there anyone I felt safe enough with to ask this question? Was it even the right question?

"I'll see what I can do." He turned coolly and efficiently, clipboard to chest, off to another patient, another family, another condition demanding his immediate attention in this complex maze of cold hospital hallways.

My father died the next morning before the paperwork came through. It was not a pretty death. It didn't resemble the deaths I've seen on TV, with a loving family gathered around the bedside, quiet music playing in the background, a soft haze enveloping the room.

The respirator was clicking rhythmically. Damn that respirator. In and out. Click. Click. Click. It sounded even louder and its clatter seemed to mock and scorn us now. I placed my hand over my dad's left hand; I was shocked and startled and I jerked it away momentarily; his own hand was cold and had turned blue. Where had all his blood gone?

The doctor was there. The chaplain was there. We were there. The doctor pronounced him dead. Nothing about his condition appeared to have changed and I wondered how they knew he had died. They unhooked him from the respirator even as the machine continued to spurt and gurgle; I was reminded of how many times over the past fifteen days I'd wanted to rip that machine from the wall and throw it out the nearest window or through the nearest wall. I was finding it hard *not* to be angry about everything that was happening. There seemed to be nothing more to do, nothing more to say. We turned for the last time and walked out of the unit, shoulders bent, eyes wet, feet leaden. The respirator's odd sound accompanied us down the hall.

Snippets of other conversations related to my dad's death float into my consciousness from time to time. All have been life-changing for me. In my mind's eye, I see the operating room nurse coming down to us after they'd brought my dad into the operating room the second time. She said, "This particular heart surgeon is known to be . . ." She paused momentarily, struggling with how to say the next part, " . . . particularly aggressive when it comes to his patients, sometimes too much so." We were left to read between those lines.

Then there was me, approaching my spiritual director, my heart bared and earnestly asking, "I don't know what to pray for. Do I pray for a cure? Do I pray for a swift and painless death? What do I pray for?" I was afraid that I was missing an opportunity to "save" my dad. If I prayed for him to live, would God hear me and answer? I didn't know. I was tormented by my unknowing. I watched my prayer evolve into this: "Help my dad to see you in every moment. Help us all to see you in every moment. Even as my dad's flesh is slowly rotting inch by wretched inch." To this day, this "Help us to see you, know you, experience you, love you" remains my primary form of prayer, for me and for all whom I love.

Another snippet. My dad's close friend, Doris, a cardiac nurse, confiding in me: "They never should have operated on your father. His heart muscle was shot." She'd seen his records; she knew what she was talking about. But what kind of choice did my dad really have? Persuasions to do "whatever it takes" can be subtle and manipulative, even when they're motivated by love and care. When the doctors recommended bypass surgery, had they offered alternatives? Had they said that "no treatment" was as viable an option as treatment? Had my father been truly free to choose? I wasn't part of the decision-making process for his surgery, so I don't have answers to these important questions.

A recent article in *The New York Times*[7] addressed this issue—but didn't seem to go far enough. So much boils down to money, the writer says: "Paying for only one session and the completion of advance directives would have limited value . . . ." Reimbursement rates for *talking*, it turns out, are much lower than for medical procedures. Pressures that thwart our efforts to improve our medical system come from other places, too. A patient reported that she "felt pressured to agree to a feeding tube because a doctor said, 'What are you trying to do, kill your husband?'" She eventually removed the feeding tube and her husband died. I shook my head in dismay as I read this, praying that this particular doctor was simply having a bad day.

The cultural sea change we desperately need to alter our attitudes around death, dying, and medical intervention seems nearly impossible. I don't know if official, sanctioned, insurance-covered end-of life talks would have helped my family avoid the heinous debacle that happened with my dad. In another article that originally appeared on Kaiser Health News, writer Jenny Gold informs us, "Medical schools are currently required to cover end-of-life care as part of their curriculum, but they offer an average of just 17 hours of training over all four years. And end-of-life care is *not* one of the crucial 15 topic areas for Step 3 of the medical licensing exams, the final step to becoming a practicing physician."[8] I was not encouraged.

---

7 Pam Belluck, "Coverage for End-of-Life Talks Gaining Ground," *The New York Times* (August 31, 2014): A1, http://www.nytimes.com/2014/08/31/health/end-of-life-talks-may-finally-overcome-politics.html?_r=0 (accessed January 4, 2016).

8 Jenny Gold, "Dying in America Is Harder Than It Has to Be, IOM Says," Kaiser Health News (September 17, 2014): 1, http://khn.org/news/institute-of-medicine-says-dying-in-america-is-harder-than-it-has-to-be/ (accessed January 4, 2016).

However, these two articles stirred my thinking and imagination even more, giving rise to other thought-provoking questions. How often are treatment options offered to a patient on a neutral playing field? What would a neutral playing field look like? I envision a space where a dying patient is told that there is no *one* right way to proceed, no *one* right decision to make. The "right" one is the one grounded in freedom and love, not the one that emanates from a place of fear, regret, or pressure. The "right" choice is the one that is most life-giving for the patient—and this life-giving parameter in the context of death is not an impossible oxymoron. A life-giving decision will bring peace, spaciousness, clarity, deeper connection to the "One," to "God," to "the All." A life-giving choice will open the doors even further into Celtic thin space, into the other "realm," into the "fourth dimension." A life-giving decision manifests and reflects the deep, deep sacredness of all that is.

What the "right" individual choice *won't* do is eliminate the pain, the tragedy, the sadness that are part of death's makeup. It won't give the dying person or his or her family and friends a fairy-tale ending. It's not about playing Pollyanna and her "glad game." Given the choice between the fairy-tale ending and the promise of a deeper connection to the sacred, the holy, the beautiful, I can only be true to myself and my values when I choose the path of connection.

Death can be incredibly beautiful. I have been generously blessed to witness so much beauty in dying. It can also be horrific. It seems important to acknowledge, and when possible, to embrace both.

I read a very moving opinion piece in the Sunday *New York Times* one Father's Day, about the death of the writer's eighty-one-year-old dad, who lived alone, died unexpectedly, and was found after he'd been dead for three days. Decay had set in and he was not a pretty sight. The author concluded: "Seeing my father's lifeless body that day was the biggest shock of my life, but it was also his last lesson to me, and it didn't come from a book or a lecture: 'This is what death looks like, son. It doesn't come with your hands pre-folded, wearing your best suit and your hair combed.'"[9] My dad could have spoken those very words to me. The only thing I would change is the absolute nature of the statement; my experience would move me to modify and say, "This is what *some* deaths look like." Some, not all, because I have witnessed absolute beauty in the dying process.

My dad's experience of rotting to death on a respirator for fifteen tortuous days taught me two things beyond any doubt: there are worse things than dying and there are far worse things than being dead.

---

9 John Max, "My Father, Body and Soul," *The New York Times* (June 15, 2014): SR5, http://www.nytimes.com/2014/06/15/opinion/sunday/my-father-body-and-soul.html (accessed January 4, 2016).

FOUR

Bookends

Life has two bookends—birth and death. They uphold and maintain order to the myriad experiences that accumulate between them. They have much in common—they happen to everyone. Nobody opts out of either. They are equally dramatic, no matter the circumstance, and they're somewhat unpredictable. A new life enters when it pleases—even with a "due date," birth has a mind of its own. And the death bookend can show up at any time. But the two phenomena also have radical differences.

It seems I never have enough bookends to go around. In my household, bookends behave sometimes like socks: I often end up with one missing. The results have been neither pretty nor effective. I've tried artfully angling the last book or two to hold the rest, but it never proves to be a permanent fix. Sometimes the process of collapse happens gradually, as the books slowly slide down an inch at a time until the whole stack is in disarray, haphazardly creeping across the shelf like a wayward, tangled, overgrown vine. Sometimes it happens with a crash that would wake the soundest sleeper. Kaboom!

We need two bookends for things to work as they're intended; we need two bookends to achieve harmony and beauty; we need two bookends to achieve and maintain balance.

One of my finest lessons and reminders about the importance of balance came from an unexpected place. My husband and his business partner started their engineering consulting firm when they were in their late twenties. To me, it felt like a bold and scary venture. But thirty-five years later the business is still thriving, and has provided us with a steady income and financial security, and most of my fears have been quelled. I've helped manage the office on and off through these years; one of my first tasks was to procure an artificial, table-top Christmas tree complete with lights and ornaments. I had a great time doing it, lugging our own small babies around, choosing everything just so. For me, the tree became a personal symbol of our success, a statement that we really were making it, and I felt a legitimate pride in that.

I chose a set of six small wooden ornaments, each picturing a child doing something. One was a seesaw on which both children were suspended, not quite level with each other, legs dangling. Each ornament included a thin red loop similar to embroidery floss. The loop on the seesaw broke early in its life as an ornament and I couldn't bear to throw it out—it was just too cute. But there seemed to be no way to reattach the thread or make a new loop.

So the Christmas tree ornament became a decoration for my desk, where it's lived for at least twenty-five years. First, it served as a visual reminder of the hours I spent as a child on a seesaw. Always, the best part of the experience happened when my friend and I were in perfect balance. It was well worth the effort it took. With none of our feet quite touching the ground, I felt like we were in some sort of mystical suspension. Seesaws, by their very nature, are delicate, sensitive, and responsive. There is an exquisite beauty inherent in the balance point. The gentle movements our bodies create when we shift our weight even the tiniest amount couldn't be replicated anywhere else on earth.

And the reverse is true: There's nothing worse than picking a mischievous—or worse, nefarious—partner to ride with you. The exquisite beauty you both so delightfully achieved a moment ago can be destroyed in seconds. If your partner decides to take a good bounce at the moment his or her feet make contact with the ground, you know you're in trouble. Zing! Before you can react, your "friend" has sent you flying into space, out of breath and maybe even a little scared, holding onto your seat for dear life. Conversely, if you're at the top, you can bounce, too, especially if you weigh more, sending your partner plummeting to the ground. Boom! Those rusty paint-chipped metal seesaw seats of my childhood provided no padding and there was usually a somewhat vociferous "ouch" attached to that particular landing. If your friend wanted you to suffer, there wasn't much you could do about it.

So many lessons have I gleaned over the years from this little ornament. Balance. Not dangling precariously in the air with no way to come down. Not stuck on the ground with no way to come up. Balance. It meant *neither* up *nor* down, but between—resting in the middle of both. Balance. It has an exquisite beauty that's critically important, personally and communally. It requires cooperation with and agreement among all the elements involved. "Yes, this is important enough for me and for you and for all involved to set aside our own personal agendas for the sake of the harmony that balance will bring us." Balance. It involves trust that the space in the middle is a place of symphonic vibration, valuable enough to let go of *my* need to control or exert *my* power over another. And it brings with it the exquisite pain of impermanence—the balance can be disrupted at any given moment.

That little broken Christmas ornament has an infused wisdom that continues to help me remember what's important, desirable, joyous: the experience of balance. On days when I'm rushing, lost, crushed by the tasks that lay ahead of me, my eyes fall on that tiny wooden sculpture. It's become my steadfast, faithful compass. I pick it up and cup it in my hands and simply gaze; it always helps me find my way back to breath and life and wholeness. Some of the words that Merriam-Webster online associates with balance are: stability, equality, aesthetically pleasing, steadiness, equipoise—a delightful word I hadn't heard until I looked up "balance." The death bookend balances the birth bookend. We need both for life to work well. The bookends bring beauty, harmony, a sense of security and stability. Try removing the second bookend from all your bookshelves and live—even for a short week—with the chaos that ensues.

Most of us are well prepared for the birth bookend. For birth, we have showers; we have coaches; we have the women who have gone before us and share their wisdom. The surprise shower that a dear friend gave me in the spring of 1977, three weeks before my first child was born, nearly put me into labor: Heart beating over a swollen belly, sweating, I was grateful for the new breathing techniques I'd learned in our Lamaze classes. I think it was a full fifteen minutes after the loud "Surprise!" was shouted before I was able to peel myself off the ceiling and my heart had returned to normal.

It was a small shower—a few friends, my mother-in-law, and several of her friends. Her friends were the most important—a generation older, they were the "elders" of the moment, seasoned moms who could tell the stories my generation was hungering to hear—needed to hear—stories of labor, delivery, umbilical cords, diapers, burping, colic, sleepless nights, the joys and the demands of new motherhood. The stories swam around the room more quickly than spring minnows in a shallow pond. My mother-in-law and her friends, who'd given birth many times, could tell us about their children being born with great detail, relish, and enthusiasm. Listening to them, we were sure they'd all given birth just yesterday, so vivid were their recollections. Some tears, some pain, but the ending was nearly always the same: there was nothing like holding your brand-new baby for the very first time. We mothers-to-be and new mothers listened intently. We could feel our excitement growing like a carefully banked fire.

While we may not remember our actual births, many of us have heard the stories at least once. My own mother labored greatly for almost a day and a half before the doctors gave her the disappointing news that a Caesarian would be necessary. As she told me later, her relief at that moment was greater than her disappointment. Her story became part of my story, one I tell with sadness because I'm always aware of how much she suffered giving birth to me. And one that I tell with joy because her suffering ended and she gave me the precious gift of life.

The death bookend is radically different. It seems a heavy weight with no substance, no shape, no open door to let us in. No one is here to tell us the stories of what death is like. We have coaches, but they coach from this side of the experience, not the other. Plus, we're only just beginning to talk about death in a way that isn't a conversation-stopper. Most of the time, if we have the courage to bring up the topic, it isn't long before someone has changed it back to the weather; even politics or religion are better choices. Anything but death.

I feel this loss, this missing piece even though I know the topic of death remains, for the most part, off limits in most circles. The father of one of the girls in my all-girls' high school died; I don't know how long he'd been dead, but I remember that her status living in a fatherless household set her apart. She began to date a guy from our brother high school whose father had also died. We viewed them both as different, strange, not like us, which is the one dreaded category every high school student lives to avoid. She'd share with us some of their conversations; she couldn't believe her fortune at having found a comrade, someone she could talk to. She fueled our fire, unbeknownst to her, by letting us know that they'd talk about their *dead* parents. We, of course, had unanimously decided that she was weird; he was weird; they were both weird; and we'd whisper behind their backs, "What is *wrong* with them?"

I'm not proud that I scorned her and played a part in building up her status as a pariah, an untouchable. I share this story because I continue to be puzzled nearly fifty years later by my own attitude. Where did it come from? How did I—and all of my friends—become so horrified, critical, judgmental, perhaps outraged about the fact that our friend had finally found someone with whom she could share her own pain and loss? At fourteen, my attitude was solid and unshakable. You didn't talk about death, and if you did, something was seriously wrong with you.

By then, I'd already been touched intimately by death—my father's mother had died when I was eight. I remember grown-ups talking in somber, hushed tones, coming and going, arranging for babysitters, dressed up in the middle of the day. How odd it had seemed to my inexperienced mind. My mother's father had died in the same year, but he was one of the black sheep in the family and not much was made of his passing. My friend's father had died tragically when I was fourteen, and a year later, that same friend died in a terrible car accident.

And even with that exposure, I and all of my peers knew that it was terribly wrong to talk about death. We hadn't been invited to consider it one of the treasured bookends of life at that point. Rather, our culturally ingrained inability to engage in conversations about it had made this bookend invisible, unknown, and obscure.

Perhaps part of the void here had to do with the prevailing person-ification of death many of us had been given—that of the Grim Reaper. William Harris, writing for the website "science.howstuffworks.com," makes a great deal of sense when he writes:

> *Clearly, what happens as we die, as well as what happens af-ter we die, is a major concern, as it has been for thousands of years. To make sense of dying and mortality, humans rely on a tried-and-true method: They give death a form they recognize. This turns an abstract, invisible phenomenon into something real and tangible. If you look at death and see a familiar face, you can understand it. If you look at death and see a kind, gentle face, even better—you can put aside your fears.*
>
> *Of course, it can work the other way. You can find a terrifying countenance when you look upon death . . .* [11]

Over the centuries, several kind faces and images have been associ-ated with death. Thanatos was the god of non-violent death. Remain-ing faithful to the principle of balance, the Greeks also had goddesses of violent death, the Keres. In Christianity, the angels Michael and Gabriel (among others) escort those who have died into the afterlife. The Muslim tradition describes Azrael as the angel who helps separate the soul from the body. Other traditions name other angels who aid and support this natural, essential passage and transformation. Death

11 William Harris, "How the Grim Reaper Works," How Stuff Works, http://science.howstuffworks.com/science-vs-myth/strange-creatures/ grim-reaper1.htm (accessed January 4, 2016).

has not only been portrayed as grim, but these other, more positive images are not as prevalent. Nor do they seem to have the same staying power or allure as that of the Reaper.

Images of the Grim Reaper, with scythe in one hand, holding the hourglass of time in the other, black-hooded cloak revealing a skull for its head, began to show up in art and word during the time of the plagues that wiped out between 30 and 60 percent of Europe's population between 1346 and 1353. Other plagues have occurred in nearly every century since then. Harris describes the effect:

> *Fear—of dying, of the unknown pestilence, of the pain associated with the late stage of the disease, when the skin on a victim's extremities turned black and gangrenous—gripped the entire continent. A general mood of morbidity hung over all activities and influenced writers and painters of the time.*[11]

It seems to me that we've yet to recover from this dark, macabre, sinister image of death. But our focus isn't to eliminate the dark; it's to provide images to balance the dark with kind and helpful images. The Greeks were wise enough to know that.

I can't have the same connection and intimacy with anyone who has died that I have with my mother, who gave birth to me. My beloved grandmother died in 1979 when I was twenty-eight. At nearly eighty-seven, she was a strong and vibrant woman who'd gone out to have her hair done the morning she died. She didn't drive, so she would've either taken the bus or called a cab to get to the salon. We'll never know. I don't even know who found her, but whoever it was found her dead, collapsed on the dining room floor of her three-bedroom apartment that very afternoon. When I tell the story, I'll often

11 Ibid.

say, "She checked out looking good," with a thin, fragile chuckle and a slight shake of my head.

My fragility stems from the fact that I can't weave my grandmother's perspective into this important story. It's an irksome gap because I can't relay to anyone, especially to my own heart, what she felt, experienced, remembered. The intimacy I feel with my mom around the story of my birth isn't possible around the story of my grandmother's death. The dead don't speak; the dead can't tell their tales. I can't quote her; I can't tell you what it was like at the moment of her passing. I can't tell you if she uttered a word or sang a hymn, or danced across the threshold. I can't tell you if her eyes were wide open or if she was paralyzed with fear of the unknown. I like to imagine that she was singing her favorite hymn, one that we sang at her memorial service, "How Great Thou Art," as her soul made its way. This missing piece of my grandmother's life is a great loss for me.

Is it any surprise, then, that those of us who are dying live in a vacuum? We're searching for information, hungry for any tidbit that might find its way to us. We're writing our own scripts, a strange thing to learn how to do. We venture into virgin territory that isn't on many maps. We get lost. We make it up day by day. We carve the death bookend by ourselves, and we have few instructions to follow or patterns from which to start. We probably wouldn't recognize death as the second, equally important bookend of life even if it were patiently pointed out to us again and again. The only value most of us can assign to death is a negative one. Our hearts dearly long for someone to come back to tell those of us who are in the throes of dying what it was like. Just one.

Tell me, Grandma, were you singing?

FIVE

The Other Side of the Coin

Behold, I am doing a new thing; now it springs forth, do you not
perceive it?
—ISAIAH 43:19 (ENGLISH STANDARD VERSION)

For at least twenty of the twenty-five years I've been a spiritual director, one of the tools in my toolbox has been the concept and experience of "both/and." In a session with a directee, I listen carefully for the often raucous collision of what appears to be complete opposites in a person's life. Suddenly, even the most open, balanced individual has slipped into the dark, rigid, and unforgiving territory of black and white. Experience has revealed to me that this is where the sacred often appears to have gone missing. Ironically, these situations are also the ones where we most need clarity and connection with the sacred.

A common way I've experienced how "either/or" thinking usurps the "both/and" looks like this: "My son has been arrested for shoplifting" followed by "I'm a good mother . . . aren't I? Maybe I'm not, 'cause if I were . . . ." If the first statement were true, the person has often decided that the second could not possibly be. So if her son has been arrested, the woman sitting across from me has begun to doubt the truth of the goodness of her motherhood. I'd offer the suggestion that both could be true. I might say something like this: "Just because your son was arrested doesn't mean you're not a good mother. The challenge is to hold these two truths at the same time, to begin to pay attention to what happens when you do."

Often, this suggestion would have a profound effect on my directee; it was humbling to be in the presence of the transformation that would begin to happen. She'd stop, she'd consider, she'd try to begin to allow both to be—a son's arrest and a deep knowing that she was a good mother. She knew in her heart she was doing everything she could to take care of her children. But her son's arrest had created a fragility and vulnerability; her sense of being a good mom had begun to erode and fall apart. Where certitude had once supported her and carried her through challenging times, doubt had begun to fill the cracks.

The two things that were essential to this situation were that (1) both statements were true, and (2) at least on a feeling level, they appeared to be in opposition with each other. It's understandable that agonizing tension could easily arise within the person's heart and soul under those conditions: if one were true, the other couldn't possibly be. In working with this woman, I'd draw two circles that were just barely touching, explaining that both experiences were true and were part of her, so they would at least be touching. My rudimentary diagram looked like this:

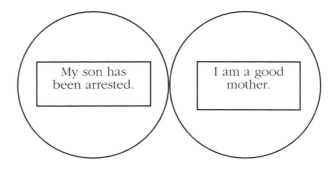

I'd then suggest that it might be helpful to see if we could somehow begin to bring those two realities together, like this:

As this understanding began to manifest itself, she began to know the truth of *both*: *Yes*, her son was arrested and *yes*, she was a good mother. She'd begun to glimpse the mandorla space. Our hope was that, in seeing the overlap, she'd also be able to dwell there. Bringing these seemingly opposite realities together would open her up to a new world of possibility—not just this, not only that, but *both*. Something new and critical to her own—and her family's—wellbeing would emerge, carrying with it a wholeness and strength not possible when the two are separated, or when one is embraced and the other is discarded.

Therapist and writer Brian Jensen describes it this way: "The mandorla is the divine container in which new creation begins to form and germinate."[12]

Many years after I'd been using this "both/and" approach in my practice, I stumbled on the Venn diagram and websites that explained

12 Brian Jensen, "Mandorla: Ancient Symbol of Wholeness," *Sandplay: The Sacred Journey* (Spring 1997).

the vesica piscis, another name for the mandorla. The vesica piscis is a shape formed by the intersection of two circles with the same diameter, intersecting such that the center of each circle lies on the perimeter of the other. The name literally means the "bladder of a fish" in Latin.

Without knowing it, I'd been working with an ancient form that connected me to the world of sacred geometry, a system that many major religions respected and included in some form in their artwork, practice, writings, and architecture. (One fine example of this is the Chalice Well cover, the holy well at the foot of Glastonbury Tor in Somerset, England). You can look at a photograph of this cover online.[13]

To create a mandorla, the two circles must contain information that's both true and seemingly opposite. The particular circles we'll look at address people's relationship with death, and we'll start with three circles. To begin, the relationships I've placed within these circles are often classified as primarily negative, difficult, or undesirable. Each relationship also has what I'd call a prevailing energy or vibration that feeds and sustains it:

The first group (1) includes those who can't say the word "death," can't talk about it, are terrified of it. The prevailing energy and foundation for the relationship would be fear.

The second group (2) includes those who view it as a mistake, a failure, something wrong that isn't supposed to happen. The prevailing energy and foundation for this relationship would be despair.

The third set of folks (3) mourns and weeps. Mourning is neces-

---

13 Available at http://www.crystalinks.com/glastonburytor.html (accessed January 4, 2016). I would invite readers to explore further should their curiosity be piqued. I am hoping that this brief background will suffice to begin an exploration of this "both/and" phenomenon; I will refer to this phenomenon by its formal names, "mandorla" and "vesica piscis."

sary, hard work. But it's easy to stop there—or worse, get stuck—without realizing it. The prevailing energy and foundation for the relationship would be grief.

So let's look at what constitutes the relationships depicted within these three circles:

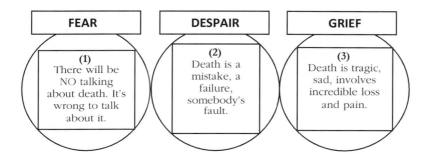

Each circle must contain true statements. Christina Feldman, in *Compassion: Listening to the Cries of the World*, cites an ancient Sufi tradition that poses three questions to help a person discern what to pay attention to and what to disregard.[14] These questions are: (1) Is the thought true? (2) Is it necessary? and (3) Is it rooted in love and kindness? Based on these criteria, it's easy to eliminate the first two circles. The first circle is simply untrue. How can it be *wrong* to talk about death even though it's an attitude that Western culture continues to promote in covert, unspoken ways? I don't quite understand how this stance is actually conveyed although, as noted in Chapter 5 of Feldman's book, Grim Reaper images underlay and sustain some of the terror. Silence can be an effective tool to prevent change, positive or negative. We're all susceptible to "magical thinking," and we may trick ourselves into believing that if we don't talk about it, perhaps it

14 Christina Feldman, *Compassion: Listening to the Cries of the World* (New York: Rodmell Press, 2005), 89.

won't happen, it isn't real, or it will go away. The fear that drives this relationship is very powerful in terms of how it influences our health care and end-of-life choices.

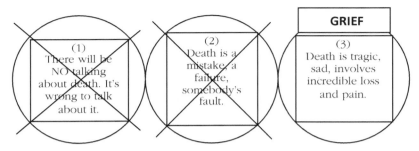

Part of this sense of failure derives from the way we describe the death of someone, especially when the cause is cancer. We often hear—or even more commonly read in the obituary—that a person who has died from cancer has "lost the battle." Losing a battle implies failure, and shows that someone or something is at fault. Could a different move on the chess board ten plays back have resulted in a win? We find it hard to resist this seductive line of reasoning. No one likes to lose, no one likes to be called a failure, and no one wants others pointing accusatory fingers accompanied by the biting words, "It's your fault you lost the battle: you should've gotten that second opinion." "It's the doctor's fault—he should've known this wouldn't work." "It's my fault—I should've made you go to the doctor sooner." This stance is especially troubling for anyone who's endured treatment for anything, either as a patient, a friend, or family member.

Our understanding that death is failure seems nearly unshakable. It's as though our ability to name the source of the failure—or, better yet, fix it—will magically bring our loved ones back to life. "Zap! You're not dead any longer. We found the cause of the failure and you're going to live." If we realize how ludicrous and impossible this is, we tell ourselves, "If it won't bring our loved ones back to life, at least maybe we can keep someone else from dying."

Not long after my father died, my mother, who cared faithfully for him throughout the twenty years he had heart disease, declared to me, "I could've done more." She'd shaved him when he was told he couldn't lift his arms above his heart after his coronary in 1968. She'd watched his diet carefully, sometimes too diligently for his liking. She'd let him know when he was overdoing it. At times her care ended up looking like nagging; her unchecked fear of his death compelled her anxious interventions. She was a nurse; she knew what to look for when he wasn't feeling well. She encouraged and supported the lifestyle changes his medical conditions demanded.

I wanted to meet her despair gently: "Oh, Mom, like what?" She looked downward, shaking her head back and forth because she knew there was no answer that would alleviate her distress, her grief. What she wanted was a magic pill that she hadn't been able to find that would've allowed my dad to live forever—not just into his eighties or nineties, but *forever*. He was considered way too young by any standards to have died at sixty-six. The fact that living forever is impossible simply does not enter into the conversation. I said, putting my arm around her tenderly and blinking back the hot tears, "Mom, you did everything you could." Sometimes it's just time to die, I thought to myself. It's that stark, that true, that painful. And that hard to accept.

I often think about how our hair grows. When we go to the hairdresser to get it cut or styled, we don't think in terms of our hair failing us because it's grown. It's not our fault that our hair needs cutting; it's not our hairdresser's mistake; it's not an oversight on the part of our best friend. Hair grows. We expect it to grow—it's the most natural thing in the world. And people die. These things are the most natural things in the world. What keeps us from accepting this reality of death? Neither death nor hair growth can be avoided. Death is also not a fault, failure, mistake, or oversight. We seem to have an almost unnatural stance toward death, a stance that separates death from life, even though they're inseparable, even though death is the second bookend of life.

After my mother died, I found myself in a serious and surprising conversation with a colleague. She was more than ten years younger than I and wise beyond her years. I was lamenting the fact that my mother was dead. Dead.

"I can't believe my mother died, Kath. Honest to God, she went through so much stuff in her life. She was sick with so many things, she'd had a million surgeries—well, maybe not quite a million—and she struggled on and off with mental illness and alcoholism her whole adult life. I just thought she'd live to be a ripe old lady—at least into her eighties. It never occurred to me that she would die so young. Kathy, she was only seventy. Think of that—*barely* seventy!" My voice, trailing off slightly into a whine, also conveyed my grief.

"Oh, Susan." She was full of compassion in that moment, but her voice was also firm and clear. "You didn't think your mom would live to be an old lady. You thought she would live forever." There it was again—only I was saying it this time about my mom rather than my mom saying it about my dad. Kathy stopped; that was all she had to say. The period at the end of that very short sentence was like the sharp end of a well-honed filleting knife, so smoothly did it slip into my heart as it took my breath with it.

My mouth dropped open, forming a big cavernous "O" shape that often happens when the truth plummets down from the heavens and rips through us like an artillery shell. I felt like I'd just been hit with a Bomb of Reality, and it was shattering. Until she'd said it, I hadn't realized that this really was what I thought, what I believed, what I'd fervently held on to for years and years. My mom would live forever. So would yours. And yours. Just ask me and I was absolutely certain of this particular facet of Truth about Death. The absurdity of that belief escaped my rational mind completely until this very wise woman named and stripped the veil from my illusion.

Death is not a mistake. It is not a failure. It is usually not somebody's fault. And it happens to everyone. No one lives forever.

The glaring truth is that the death of a loved one is sad, tragic, hard, beyond comprehension, gut-wrenching, horrible, shocking when it is sudden and even when our loved ones have been sick for a long time. These responses are as natural (and important) as death itself. But what remains of our three-circle diagram is a single, isolated circle. Every coin has two sides, and we have only filled in one. So we can't create a mandorla; we can't unleash the sacred power of the overlapping circles; we can't tap into their symbolic power; we can't enter into its promise of "something new" because we need a second circle to form the mandorla.

Not just the importance but the stark necessity of this second circle became even clearer when I remembered a story I hadn't thought of in a very long time.

While I was in college I accidentally overwore my contact lenses. This led to a painfully scratched cornea, a costly visit to an ophthalmologist on a college student's limited budget, and a bulky white patch over the affected eye for many days. The result was monocular vision— with one eye blacked out, you lose your depth perception, among other things. Unfortunately, I wasn't aware of that particular effect then.

One morning, eye patch securely taped to forehead and cheek bone, I was happily making a poached egg; the water had just come to the requisite boil, the bread was in the toaster, everything was ready. I approached the stove, egg in hand, and cracked it sharply on the edge of the pan. I then went to drop it into the water, and I ended up with my hand in the boiling water! No depth perception, hand burned slightly, a little wiser, a little more careful.

If we only see out of one eye, we see with distortion and inaccuracy; we risk exposing ourselves to unnecessary danger. We're less than a breath away from plunging into boiling water and getting burned beyond recognition. When my mother-in-law died (the last of our parents to die in a little more than six years), I was bereft. Beside myself. I sought counseling to deal with a grief that felt like it would overtake me at any moment—I was suffocating, drowning, floundering; I felt like I would die of a grief-stricken heart. I feared I wouldn't recover.

I was certain that a focused, determined, and very smart octopus had reached out from the depths of my being, firmly attached all eight of its arms to my legs, and was rapidly pulling me into a dank place from which I wouldn't emerge. All I knew in those first agonizing months was that death was tragic, sad, and involved incredible loss and pain. I needed more than that perspective if I were to recover my wholeness, my balance, and my sacred light.

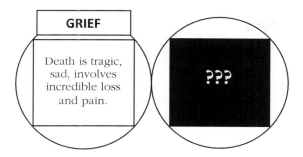

Then I was blessed with a miracle that took the form of a conversation whose origins come from that mysterious "other" realm. I "heard" a "voice" with my inner ear. In this realm, there is no sound and no words as we would normally describe them; they are pure emanations that are true to their own origin and form. The voice asked me a question, "So, would you like to be grieving less?" I thought this was one of the most ridiculous questions I had ever been asked, in this realm or in any other.

My sarcasm overtook any good manners my mother had drilled into me and I said something like, "What do you think? Who wouldn't?" Inside the safety of my own head, I was also asking, "What kind of stupid question is that? Who in their right mind wants to grieve?"

The voice remained steady, undeterred by my scorn, and simply said, "Well, then, you would have to have loved her less." No further words were needed. I was stunned. Suddenly, my whole sense of grief changed radically; the change was so rapid and complete that, even with practice, I wouldn't have been able to snap my fingers any faster. No longer was my grief only a vehicle for misery and lament. This unembellished statement had effectively established a relationship between my grief and my love for this woman who had become a second mother to me. Love and grief were reflections of each other—if I loved, I would grieve. I wouldn't grieve if I hadn't loved. I got it.

My grief didn't lift; it no longer needed to. It became purposeful, another way to understand and express the depth of my love for her and hers for me. In so doing, it became tolerable, no longer an enemy or an instrument threatening my extinction. It became, if not a friend, an intimate part of death, one facet of it, a symbol and sign of a deeply loving relationship that had flourished for nearly twenty-five years. Gratitude began to well up inside my worn and aching heart.

Thus began my understanding of and my ability to talk about death as a both/and experience. It *is* sad. It *is* hard. It *is*, at times, unbearable, no matter if it is the death of a child, an adult in his or her prime, or a person who's been clinging to life on a respirator for weeks. No matter if the cause is an accident, murder, suicide, illness. It *is* impossibly hard to navigate the landscape of death with much grace when one eye is bandaged and securely taped shut.

So what does this second circle look like? What are its contents? What happens when the circles overlap and their contents begin to mingle and commingle? This overlap has been named and described in this way,

> *The vesica piscis signifies the mediation of two distinct enti-*
> *ties; the complementariness of polar opposites, as when two*
> *extremes complete and depend upon one another to exist. One*
> *circle may signify the breath of spirit, which is eternal; the oth-*
> *er may signify the body physical, which is forever changing*
> *and adapting. The vesica piscis itself symbolizes that which*
> *mediates spirit; or the psyche or soul.*[15]

15 Randall Carlson, "The Meaning of Sacred Geometry Part 3: The Womb of Sacred Geometry," http://sacredgeometryinternational.com/the-meaning-of-sacred-geometry-part-3-the-womb-of-sacred-geometry (accessed January 4, 2016).

Over the past nine years, I've experienced primary breast cancer, my husband's prostate cancer, my son's suicide, and now advanced primary lung cancer, which will probably cause my death, sooner rather than later. During this time, I've been blessed with many fine teachers, guides, and companions. With their generous help and wisdom and a great deal of prayer and meditation, I've come to catch glimpses of this second circle. Accompanied by this critical second eye, and with circles that overlap to create the sacred inner mandorla, death reveals itself to be necessary; to be natural; to be a form of completion; and to possess an inherent beauty. The communication from the other realm had clearly revealed that this aspect of the relationship with death is grounded in love.

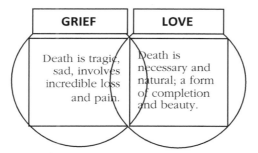

GRIEF	LOVE
Death is tragic, sad, involves incredible loss and pain.	Death is necessary and natural; a form of completion and beauty.

This is not meant to diminish, ignore, or pretend that death isn't incredibly painful. We can't have one circle without the other. The sacred space where they overlap in the middle allows everything to change. This configuration provides us with much-needed balance. It creates a sense of solid ground underneath our feet, an experience of sacred connection that's inclusive and abandons none of our experience, is as alive and real as breathing is real. This side of the coin can be felt and experienced as a type of living being that seeks and longs to support us straight through the full experience of death. When I contemplate this type of support, I fill with gratitude and the blessings seem endless. The end of the fifth verse of Psalm 23, which is often proclaimed at funerals, has never been more alive for me or held more meaning: "My cup overflows."

SIX

Loss

Although the types of losses that are most commonly experienced with terminal illness don't happen all at once, these days many of my little and mighty accomplishments have often felt like dominoes proudly *and* precariously lined up on the dining room table. Some unseen force would begin to shake the first, and immediately the whole lot of them became a noisy, raucous cascade that came crashing down in pieces. Loud, painful, and wrenching, the sound was always an intrusion, an unwanted sign of my pending death. Before we can fully explore what death means in terms of being necessary, natural, complete, and beautiful, it is imperative to also talk about what the other circle looks like—the circle of nearly insufferable loss, pain, brokenness. And while the particular losses I am writing about are not about the death of a particular person, they are about the deaths of cherished parts of my body and life that happen as I have drawn closer to physical death.

The clearest loss I've had to date as a result of my cancers is my mastectomy in May 2006. At my final post-surgery check-up, I was given a two-and-a-half-page pathology report—neatly typed and filled with a technical language that I'd learned to tentatively but proudly interpret with an amateur's level of familiarity. This curling, thin, slightly wrinkled copy paper was the only thing that remained of my left breast. Had my breast thinned, curled, and wrinkled, too, as the surgeon had removed it, I wondered? I had donated the tissue to research so I imagined that it had been dissected and placed carefully on slides, neatly labeled and categorized, scattered to various labs studying the myriad aspects of breast cancer causes and cures. My familiar image of this breast that had served me so well no longer matched its current, harsh, and cold reality.

My surgeon was pleased and satisfied—no cancer in the seven lymph nodes they had removed and the small tumor that was found in my breast had good, "clean" margins, the kind that encourage oncologists. I left the hospital holding the report in my hand, feeling strangely numb. I wanted to be delighted—the report meant no more surgery, no radiation; the surgeon had carefully reassured me of that. Formal treatment of this cancer was *over*.

Instead of feeling appropriately encouraged and reassured, I felt empty, as though I were looking into a great, murky, bewildering void. What was I most aware of? That everything felt different and so much harder. Had the world changed, I wondered? It sure felt like it had. I slid into the passenger seat, carefully laying my seatbelt over my right breast and the tender, jagged incision where my left breast had been. This trip to the doctor's office was my first outing since my surgery. The simple task of "buckling up" that I had once taken for granted took all my concentration and energy. I found my hand shaking with the effort, leaving me with no energy to ponder the results of my pathology report. This little trip had taken everything I had.

Then, with no warning, the tears began to flow. Not that I hadn't cried in the nine days since my mastectomy or during the nearly five months since my diagnosis. But these tears had a fierceness and a determination that surprised me. Big alligator tears. The only thing left of my breast is a two-and-a-half-page pathology report. Those words took hold in my heart and wouldn't let go. They seemed to find a voice of their own, transformed into a mantra that wasn't mocking or ridiculing, just persistent: *"The only thing left of your breast is a two-and-a-half-page pathology report."*

I could have *tried to* rationalize and reassure myself with comforting words but they'd have sounded ridiculously hollow—and they'd have been patently untrue. At that moment, I was more aware of the physical loss than I was of the good news of the report, more aware of the acute emotional loss than the reassuring memories about my breasts that had accumulated through the years. Those poignant times could not bring me even one proton of relief as my husband drove out of the parking lot. Copious tears and an agonizing absence of a part of me that I'd long held dear were all I had.

It defied my imagination that a human breast—*my* human breast—could be reduced to little specks of black ink on a white sheet of paper. Somehow, it wasn't fair or reasonable, right or just. I didn't care; the only thing that mattered at the moment was that I now had an eleven-inch angry red slash mark that started in the middle of my chest and ran all the way around, under my armpit, ending at the outside edge of my left rib cage.

All the way home, past familiar streets and stores and houses, past lawns just settling into their spring luxuriance, my tears streamed. The reflexive, quiet, 'round and 'round movement of the car's wheels provided a glaring contrast for my jumbled thoughts. My emotions felt as weighted down as the new, fresh, corpulent green buds that were weighting down tender tree limbs. I dreaded those final feet down our driveway. It meant the end of a devastating road that I had never wanted on my map. All that was left was lying on the couch that had become my command central through the eighteen grueling weeks of chemotherapy, praying for unconsciousness to overtake me.

I couldn't let go of these three pieces of paper; I couldn't stop crying. All the way through the grilled cheese sandwich my husband prepared with such care, concern, and love, hoping that he'd found the antidote that would assuage my grief. Crying as I lay down again, seeking the comfort and familiarity of my pillow, with its worn, soft yellow flannel cover. Crying through the napkin on the coffee table, and then through the one meager tissue my husband had fetched for me. Finally realizing that this was a siege over which he had no control, he set the family-sized box of Kleenex at my side. He patted my pillow lightly and remarked at how wet it was. He didn't know what else to say, how else to be, how else to express his love. This was. Loss.

My poet's pen crafted its response six months later:

Simple Mastectomy

Lying on my back,
Flat, body waking,
Fingertips probing
*   shocking horror*
Finding bone, hidden once,
safely cushioned by
*   ample breast.*

Hard ridges, narrow ribs,
empty hard hollow now
*   in the middle of my chest.*
These are bones that ache,
Skin stretched taut against them.

The star–white scar travels long,
  reveals the loss,
   the medical invasion,
    the surgeon's sharp scalpel
Scraping, scraping, scraping
every tissue remnant.

What is the sound of knife to bone?

The other losses associated with my breast cancer were the result of the six rounds of chemotherapy that I endured from January through April 2006. It seemed mildly ironic that my last chemo took place on Good Friday. The losses my body will bear until I die include permanent neuropathy in the tips of my fingers and toes; acid reflux; a mouth that's extremely sensitive to acidic foods and dressings. And strangely, I have very little body odor because, as my oncologist explained, my sweat will no longer support the bacteria that causes it. I found that a bit eerie and peculiar. Each change contributed to a growing sense that I didn't know who I was anymore. That was a much greater loss.

None of these side effects were life-threatening. However, they were inconvenient and they remain—to this day—a daily reminder of just how toxic chemotherapy is. I also knew that they meant that, no matter the method I chose to treat my terminal lung cancer, my body would begin in an already compromised position. How compromised I didn't know, but I wasn't willing to take my chances. This situation made it clearer for me to say "no, no, and no again" to any palliative treatments for my lung cancer, no matter how benign they might be billed.

The experience of loss is a complex process. It's nearly impossible to live through loss without knowing the grief that's so attached to it. Elisabeth Kübler-Ross was a pioneer in this field, publishing her now famous book, *On Death and Dying*, in 1969. Her five stages of grief: denial, anger, bargaining, depression, and acceptance became the standard by which people began to shape and evaluate their own grief. Her clearly articulated steps have helped many people regain a sense of mastery and control over a situation that had stripped them of every semblance of those things. But an article in *The New Yorker* made me think of this process a little differently. Writer Meghan O'Rourke notes that "new research suggests that grief and mourning don't follow a checklist; they're complicated and untidy processes, less like a progression of stages and more like an ongoing process—sometimes one that never fully ends."[16]

And the timeframe we put around grief and mourning is rarely adequate. How often have we said, "It's been six months; I thought she'd be over it by now, didn't you?" Or we direct the critical comments inwardly: "I should be over this by now. Come on, snap out of it!"

Loss can be uniquely personal or profoundly communal—from a couple to a family, from a neighborhood or a town, and all the way up the socio/cultural ladders that our lives span. Even with the progress we've made to willingly look at our losses and reclaim our grief, we have a long way to go. For each step we take forward into a healthier relationship with loss, grief, death, and dying, we take at least half a step back. O'Rourke shared her own story. "When my mother died, Christmas a year ago," she writes, "I wondered what I was supposed to do in the days afterward—and many friends, especially those who had

16 Meghan O'Rourke, "Good Grief: Is There a Better Way to Be Bereaved?," *The New Yorker* (February 1, 2010), http://www.newyorker.com/magazine/2010/02/01/good-grief (accessed January 4, 2016).

not yet suffered an analogous loss, seemed equally confused."[17] Many of my own losses reflect O'Rourke's confusion.

Another part of grief and loss involves commitment to the *process*, to being faithful to paying attention to its complex history; to appreciating its unpredictable momentum and rhythm. This is hard to do because our mentors are few and the topic is still off limits for most people. The commitment, naturally, is two sided: commitment on the part of the person experiencing the loss, whether he or she is dying of a terminal illness or the unfamiliar steps of the dance that death choreographs in each of our lives. The other side of the commitment is on the part of the person or group to whom the grieving person has turned to share his or her story. The grieving seek comfort and understanding, longing to be heard. John Fox has a poem entitled, "When Someone Deeply Listens to You," in which he describes what I would call the grace of deep listening.

This kind of listening is essential to our own wellbeing, and unfortunately, it is far too rare in our everyday experiences. In the context of death and dying, though, it's even more critical. Deep listening is at the core of good spiritual direction practice. I've often used the following words to describe how to hone this practice: "Time to belly up to the bar." This phrase locates the process in our bodies. Deep listening originates in our gut; it is not an intellectual endeavor. It signifies a willingness to step forward, to engage with the other person's story, to feel the bar's edge press into your belly hard, to not back away, even for an instant, even if the content of the conversation becomes raw, edgy, filled with pain. Even when the border of that bar has a sharp metal edge that's already made an indent on your soft flesh. *Especially* not then.

Often, our backing away isn't literal or physical; rarely do we

17 Ibid.

bounce back to the furthest corner of the room when a person's story has veered into waters that are so intimate that we fear for our safety and comfort. Our backing away is more subtle. We may back away by saying things like, "You know, in the end, everything will turn out OK." (One friend calls this "pious pabulum.") Or, we may say something like my friend Gloria said to me: "I knew someone who went through that same thing—let me tell you their story." Either approach minimizes or overlooks the content of the story of the person who is standing right in front of us, a flesh and blood human being who's in pain at this very moment, seeking our support. *We* may be relieved, but our friend is likely feeling forlorn, puzzled, and perhaps surprised by the rapidity with which the topic has been switched. But instead, "Belly up to the bar" is a more helpful approach. To stay, to offer an open heart and a sacred container in which this person's grief can reside, is essential. It's also hard, and it takes practice.

The losses associated with my lung cancer, while more subtle, were all irreversible. Sometimes they were devastatingly debilitating, while at others, more restrained. I found myself becoming used to the sad effects they had on the quality of daily living, especially when I was tired. Mostly, I couldn't breathe. I coughed. I was so tired. My chest hurt when I took a deep breath. The losses seemed silly sometimes—like choosing to take the elevator and not the stairs at work, knowing that this was a permanent loss; I'd never climb three flights of commercial stairs again. Or deciding that it wasn't worth going downstairs to our bedroom to get that long-sleeved shirt when the summer evening had turned unexpectedly cool. Sometimes I'd ask my husband; sometimes I'd do without. Nearly every decision revealed my slow decline.

I'd never been one to cancel things—I'd made it a matter of pride to always show up, no matter what. Lung cancer smashed that streak of pride into a million pieces as I found myself canceling dates with friends because I'd awakened feeling weak and sick. With deep dread and a heavy heart, I'd watch myself picking up the phone to break an engagement. Some of these conversations went well, but many did not. Often, a friend could not accept my "no," no matter how clearly I had stated it. "Well, maybe you'll feel better later in the day and you could come over then," they'd counter. "Maybe it would help if I visited you this time." Or they'd end the conversation with a promise to show up at my door with a plate of brownies. I knew my friends meant well; their offers and responses arose from a place of love and reflected the richness of our relationships. I also felt an ill-defined sense of pressure and I felt I hadn't communicated what was best for me. Woven into this unholy mess was my sense that I had failed to meet my friends' needs.

Sometimes, my own sadness about canceling a sweetly anticipated lunch or tea date overwhelmed me. I couldn't hold back my desolate tears long enough to finish the telephone call; I so didn't want to make my weeping a part of their day. I recognized that this familiar behavior pattern wasn't healthy; I also knew I had a great deal to learn about allowing my friends to support me through my tears. I'd often been the one to whom my friends turned when they needed comfort and a tender hug, but I found it challenging to keep up with the rapid reversal of roles.

I knew the day would come when I'd no longer even have a choice; my body simply wouldn't be able to do it. There was no "getting over" a terminal lung cancer diagnosis with the time-tested advice to get plenty of rest, drink plenty of fluids. The loss of the hope of getting better if I prudently followed the prescribed protocols was a surprisingly strange experience that I'd never had before. Loss. Loss. Loss. This loss of hope was so unexpected. I felt I'd been carelessly, cruelly jettisoned into an empty cavern so large I could see no entrance, no exit, no beginning, no ending, no escape. This was an unforgiving landscape, one I definitely did not like.

Six months after I was diagnosed, my husband and I traveled to Phoenix for his cousin's wedding. I was delighted because, in January when we received the invitation, I wasn't sure I'd be able to make it. It was an early evening wedding—the ceremony began at five-thirty in the evening on a lush green golf course as the sun bathed us all in golden light. The bride and groom proclaimed their "I do's" under a gaily festooned white wooden canopy. The reception was held on the grounds, and dinner was served around eight. By nine I was done: tired, having trouble breathing. The hotel shuttle had begun to run again for those guests like me who were turning into pumpkins even though the night was still young. Nine o'clock? I'd always loved parties, people, dancing, and laughter. I still did. But my failing body cast the deciding vote and I couldn't avoid listening to it without paying costly consequences.

I leaned over in my husband's direction and told him I needed to leave, that I'd take the shuttle back. He protested, always at the ready to be my knight in shining armor. "I'll go with you to the hotel and then I'll come back." I knew by his tone that this was no idle offer. But I insisted: "No. I need to do this by myself. And you need to do this by yourself. You need to stay with your family. That's why we're here."

Hard to explain, but we both knew that this wasn't only true but important. Without putting it into words, it felt like a dry run, a practice jog around the field, for when the time came when I really wouldn't be here, wouldn't be escorted home. Tonight, I'd be there to greet him when he walked through the hotel door. This time. And we both knew that we were running out of these "times" far more quickly than we'd have liked.

By the time I'd boarded the little shuttle and buckled my seat belt, I was already feeling bereft. I found myself sucking back the tears as fast as they threatened to unleash their unruly presence. It would've been so easy to just let it all out. But my driver—a sweet young college girl—didn't need to know about my terminal cancer, or that I'd just left my husband at the reception because I was too sick to stay. The five-minute jaunt from reception to hotel was thankfully over before I lost control, but as soon as my first foot was on the ground, the tears began. Out they flew from every nook and cranny of my being as I walked from the front of the hotel's entrance all the way around the path to our room in a different part of this maze-like complex. Into our room I threw myself, the tears washing me right over the threshold, an uncontrollable tsunami of heartache.

My hands trembling with sadness, I removed each piece of jewelry; each action was accompanied by the stark reality that I was alone because I was dying. The tears became a sweeping tidal wave. Off with my beautiful deep teal-colored chiffon cocktail dress and onto its hanger, the tears now a gyrating machine that shuddered my shoulders and quaked my heart. Into my jams, retrieving my book, tucking myself in for a read, the tears a cloying blanket I couldn't shake off.

By the time my husband returned, my tears had spent themselves. Surprising myself, I'd actually been able to read my book, and he'd had a good time with his cousins. Later, when we spoke about it, I asked him what it was like for him to stay after I left. He answered with a simplicity that conveyed far more than his words: "I was so alone."

Deep breaths all around. We'd stepped into the future for a brief moment that had been nearly unbearable and then slid gratefully back into the present where we could hug each other and offer real comfort in the face of what was happening.

Some losses are more unexpected than others and harder to put into words. After my son died, we scattered his ashes along a ridge in central Maine. It was a three-hundred-foot climb; the trail wasn't well traveled and it was fairly steep in places. The path was mostly on his property; the overlook just a little beyond that. The vista is well worth the effort: a lush, tree-filled valley broadly opens to greet you on your arrival, not a house or manmade object in sight. At the bottom of the three-hundred-fifty-foot drop is a pristine lake. My son hiked up to that ridge often, and my younger daughter took one of my favorite photos of him sitting right on its rock ledge: he's in profile on a bright October morning, oak leaves looking like coppery leather brush against the cloth of his right pant leg. He's looking intently and his dark hair is streaked with a few telltale strands of silver that glisten in the sunlight, a genetic gift we often joked about—his hair started turning in his late twenties, just as mine had, and he never failed to remind me of the "flaw" he'd inherited, to his utter dismay, from me.

There was no question of where to scatter his ashes. We hiked up the ridge on a soft, cloudy May afternoon; the buds on the trees that far north had barely begun to be tinged with that first shade of pale yellow-green. The photos show it more yellow than green; in my memory the buds are much greener than they actually were. I needed everything to feel and look alive, to be the salve that bathed the vast, dried-up, useless wasteland that had once been my heart. Gray clouds swirled in the sky, occasionally spitting misty drops of rain at us, never enough to be taken seriously. I'd only been up to the spot one other time, the Mother's Day weekend all five of us had hiked up there. It had been as beautiful as my son had told us it would be; we weren't disappointed by the hike or the view that awaited us at the lookout.

The spot was imbued with the inherent quiet of the forest that I always find deeply moving. It felt like every tree, every limb, every nascent bud, every pine needle on the forest floor, every cloud, every drop of rain, every current of air, every note of every bird song was paying attention, willingly surrendering to nature's rapture, generously giving us their support. We scattered his ashes mostly in silence. Although we'd mixed and scattered my in-laws' ashes nearly two decades previously, this task felt monumentally different and one for which we had no script. We moved slowly, deliberately, reverently.

Occasionally, we'd take a break, walking to the edge and peering over as far as our courage would take us. The dangerously long drop to the bottom gave me a brief, welcome shift away from this grief-laden task and cautioned me to take my steps with care. The view of the valley stirred my soul, bringing me a measure of comfort and drawing me into a space where the only language spoken was of beauty and harmony. The essence of it was one of unity and permeability, of a universe eager and capable of meeting me in my sorrow and sadness.

While I can only convey my experience, this little rag-tag band of mourners dressed in faded jeans or khakis and sturdy hiking shoes felt so bound together through their grief that I wasn't able to see where one of us began and another of us ended. Holy Oneness. My sense of this mysterious presence that had stealthily enveloped all of us was confirmed by a friend who accompanied us and said he'd never attended a graveside service as moving, loving, and reverent.

Six months later, on my son's birthday weekend, we walked up to the ridge again, this time to place the memorial stone that a dear friend (and stone worker) had made. He'd jokingly mentioned that we could have named him something that had fewer letters. "Matthew O'Neil Jorgensen" had been a challenge to fit on a piece of granite and we heartily agreed. Our laughter, as always, was a needed balm.

As daunting a task as it was, he'd done a marvelous job cutting and shaping the memorial.

By then, I'd been diagnosed with terminal cancer, but I needed and wanted to carry the forty-five-pound stone partway up the trail. Just as I'd joyfully carried him in my softly cushioned, happy, happy womb for nine months. Just as I'd carried, in grief, his box of ashes, pressing them into the space below my navel where I knew my womb resided. Now was the time for me to carry this part of him on my back with grit and grim determination. I had no idea my womb could change shape so facilely to suit the task that it was facing at the moment: from flesh to coated cardboard to Vermont granite.

My husband had carefully lashed the stone to one of the backpack frames we'd bought just after we'd married in 1972. Anticipating my family's objections, I'd stated quite clearly at dinner the evening before our trek that I was going to carry the stone partway, and that I'd carry it first while I still had energy. And that my decision was not—read my lips, *not*—up for family discussion. And that was that. They knew better than to try to talk their stubborn mother out of this one.

Again, the hike proved to be therapeutic and healing for all of us. We were blessed with a rainbow as we drove to my son's home, and blessed with one at his house just after we'd hiked down and stood in his yard. While we were up on the ridge, I was surprised that I could still see some of the ash that we'd scattered six months before. My cousin, looking very serious about his assigned task, had brought a concrete-cast, medieval-looking, foot-tall guardian holding a sword to protect the spot, and a dear friend had brought sawdust from his woodshop, shaped into a heart and placed next to the memorial stone. I experienced the power of an all-encompassing, loving presence scooping up each of us. The profound and ubiquitous nature of grace shows up everywhere.

Even with my cancer diagnosis, from that moment on I envisioned all of us gathering on that ridge every November to celebrate the anniversary of his birth. The sacred presence I experienced there would become our faithful anchor year after year. I didn't realize how much I'd counted on this until it dawned on me that this would never happen. First of all, our younger daughter was moving west for at least a five-year commitment. She wouldn't be there for even the first-year anniversary. And secondly, while I was becoming aware that my decline in health would prevent me from making the three-hundred-foot climb, even if I were alive, I was finding it hard to let go of an old adage that had seen me through many a tough spot: "Where there's a will, there's a way." By then, I had been on oxygen 24/7 for more than a month; even with that support, a short walk from my living room to my bathroom was leaving me breathless. Slowly, my pie-in-the-sky thinking was being indifferently stolen by the coarse, hard edges of reality.

The loss I felt was searing, a laser beam cutting into the soft flesh of my abdomen. I hadn't realized how much I'd unconsciously counted on that annual trek to renew my soul, to bring me comfort, to help me appropriate even more deeply Julian of Norwich's words, "All will be well and all manner of things will be well."[18] I told my older daughter that the energy I experienced on that ridge during our two treks up there was as strong and deeply affecting as any spiritual vortex I'd ever known. The loss of never experiencing it again was beyond my ability to grasp or comprehend.

The losses continued. One by precious one. For fifteen years, I'd had the privilege of belonging to a peer supervision group for spiritual directors. We met monthly through the academic year, and the trust, honesty,

18 *Revelations of Divine Love*, which also bears the title *A Revelation of Love—in Sixteen Shewings* (Norwich, England, 1395), Chapter XXVII.

devotion, and love among us had grown to a depth none of us had anticipated. For each of us, this professional group had become a sacred space where we could safely open ourselves up and explore difficult, sensitive issues. All of us have experienced great healing in our time together.

Six months after I received my terminal lung cancer diagnosis, I knew I wouldn't be able to continue with the group. By then I'd closed my practice and my increasingly unstable health made getting to appointments less and less reliable. It was March 2014 when I announced to the group that I'd leave at the end of that academic year. This was a tremendous jolt for all of us. June was always our last meeting, when we evaluated our year, looking at high and low points, suggesting ways to improve our time together. This year would be painfully different—we'd say our final goodbyes.

The parting hung heavy over the two hours we were together and an awkwardness arose that felt worse than the clumsiness of my first junior high school dance—I was working with a tongue tied in double knots, two left feet and sweat glands that felt like fully turned-on faucets. I'd never said goodbye under these circumstances before. Where was that playbook—complete with silver lining, please—just when I most needed it? One of us mentioned the uneasiness obliquely, "I had wondered about whether we should be planning some special way to say goodbye to Susan, I didn't know. . ." and then her voice trailed off, siphoned away by the force of the unknown and the unfamiliar.

But we chose to follow our regular format because it was important to all of us. This wasn't about avoidance or denial; it reflected our professional commitment to the integrity of our group and our process. We also knew that it provided us with a safe container from which to enter these uncharted waters of final goodbyes. I asked to go last because I knew I'd be overwhelmed by my tears.

We were making an ending. We'd all make beginnings in new ways; theirs would be without me, as mine would be without them. I lamented, "Saying goodbye to you is one of my greatest losses. When I look back through all of the people and experiences that have most influenced my life, this group—and each of you—has contributed to who I have become. I can't imagine who I would be without having known you; I can't imagine *not* being here. It has been such a privilege." By then, I was sobbing.

One of my peers interjected, "But you will be with us, Susan, you will." She was emphatic as she added, "Your spirit will always be here, every time we meet. We could never forget you. When we come back in September after our summer break, you'll be with us." She was offering me the comfort that she could in the best way she knew. Rather than comfort, however, I felt like someone was trying to steal from me the raw pain of the loss of something I held dear. "Let's just all focus on feeling good in September" was what I heard. I couldn't let that happen. I felt her comment was an attempt to divert this precious group from these final, tearful goodbyes. I was terrified that the diversion would leave me—all of us, really—emotionally stripped and isolated with our sorrows at a time we most needed the communal presence to hold us tight right now.

One of my favorite quotes around this aspect of death was written by a liturgical theologian, Gerard Sloyan, whose words I've found affirming and reassuring. I've offered them countless times to the people in my spiritual direction practice who were struggling with grief:

> *Your grief is your own, all the days of your life.*
> *Let no one deprive you of it, not even out of love.*
> *Pain is inseparable from love; that is a truth we must live with.*

It is a proof of our true inner reality, a judgment of ourselves, as to how and with what courage we face and accept that truth.[19]

I replied to my peer, as calmly and as politely as I could, "I do know that. I do. And I know you are trying to be helpful. Right now, I need to simply express how truly bereft I am. I want—and need—all of you to be there with me in the midst of this real ending. I don't need or want anyone to try to fix this right now, or make it better. I don't want anyone to try to take this pain away or make it nice. This moment right now, this group right here, and each of you are too important to me."

I had barely finished stammering and blubbering my way through this when another member chimed in, "That's right. You're sad, Susan, and your sadness is about how much you love us and we love you. We're sad, too." Her eyes were as clear as her heart was open and her words wrapped themselves around us, beholding and supporting us with a gossamer mantle of love.

We all breathed a collective sigh of relief. Her wisdom helped us stay present to the pain each of us was experiencing. How could we not hang in there after she'd given us a magnificent container of love in which to hold it and keep it sacred and protected? It also reminded me and reflected the insight I'd been given after my mother-in-law died: "Love and grief are reflections of each other—if I love, I will grieve. To avoid grief, I will have to avoid love." The connection was complete and its simplicity was stunning.

As we ended and bid our final goodbyes, copious tears and hugs swaddled us; we became infants in the arms of a loving mother whom some of us knew as God, some as Mystery, some as Presence, some as

19 Virginia Sloyan, ed., *A Sourcebook about Christian Death*, Sourcebook Series (Chicago: Liturgy Training Publications, 1990), 103.

the One and the Source. Our acknowledged loss, tenderly and public-
ly held, gently accompanied us down the stairs, out into the parking
lot, and into our cars. Each of us headed off in different directions
with heavy hearts, swathed and eternally connected by a soft blanket
of transcendent, steadfast love.

Hermit Crab in Broken Shell

We sit in polite circle.
Ten of us gather for a morning of
    reflection.
We sip brewed coffee from paper cups.
We serve up hermit crabs
to consider, to observe, to chew on.
We engage in polite conversation about
    these creatures
who will become an exemplar example
    for us.
Their shells grow too small
forcing them to move out to search for
    larger ones.
We are asked to focus
on the grace of our own "moving."

We are told that we will embark on
    what is called,
"a richly sensuous journey."
The polite nod politely
enter the metaphor eager
to suckle at its crusty breast
to express polite gratitude
for the generous invitation.
The hermit crabs move.
The conversation stretches for an eon.
The shell I am in begins to ache
and darken. I am so tiny inside.

My shell did not grow too small.
It broke.
    No.
Cancer broke it.
Chemo shattered what was left.
Surgery did away with the remains.
It was neither rich nor sensuous.

It was black. It was white.
It was cut. It was dried.
    No.
It was not polite.
I did not want to move.
I did not want a new shell.
I did not outgrow it.
I did not get to choose the new one.
    No.
Save your euphemisms for those
who have learned polite
who can't face the bleeding rawness
    of the impolite.

Poisoned. Cut up. Thrown away.
New home. Whose home? Who's
    home?
Not me. I've run away.
Peeling shutters bang shamelessly
    against darkened windows.
I prefer homelessness to this home.
Whose shriveled fingers?
Whose numb feet?
Whose fake breast?
Whose sluggish energy? Whose hair?
I did not want this new home.

We are grim-faced. Stoic.
We are sad. Bereft.
We are nearly dead.
We are not polite.

SEVEN

Necessary and Natural

Death is as necessary and natural as birth. Just like birth, it doesn't always go smoothly. Perhaps it would go smoothly more often if we learned not to fear or avoid it, if we consciously and intentionally began to teach, coach, and mentor one another about death in language that's more accessible and supportive. The children's book *Everybody Poops* by Taro Gomi has always intrigued me; a dear friend finally bought it for me. Not long after that, I discovered that the author had written a another book using a similar format and style called *Everybody Dies: A Children's Book for Grown-Ups*. Childlike drawings fill every page. The cover is a cartoon drawing of a skull with a balloon caption that has the words, "Don't feel bad." Some of the reviews of the slim volume include "macabre" and "darkly humorous." The back cover declares, in thick childlike printing, "Nobody likes to think about death, but the world would be awfully crowded without it." I actually think Taro's approach makes sense. The idea seems staggering to me, a bit silly, and quite practical. Death simply has to happen in order to make space for new life to come into being—it's a most pragmatic approach to death's necessity.

114 THIS SIDE OF HOME

Delving more deeply, Joseph Campbell in *The Power of Myth* describes death in this way:

> *The conquest of the fear of death is the recovery of life's joy. One can experience an unconditional affirmation of life only when one has accepted death, not as contrary to life but as an aspect of life. Life in its becoming is always shedding death.*[20]

If we desire life and living life to its fullest, we can only view death as necessary. Without it, we risk reducing life to an unattached broken shadow of itself.

Three of my own life experiences stand out in terms of understanding the necessity of death. My first experience took place less than thirty-six hours after my son died. It was early morning on the rocky coast of Maine. I was sitting on a park bench, contemplating the silver-gray of the ocean, which was completely flat at that time of day. Nature had become the master ironer, deftly removing every ripple, swell, and current from the water that stretched itself out lazily and languidly. Its quiet, smooth spirit drew my eyes further and further outward to the point where the sky, the same silver-gray, met it. Everything in the universe seemed to be absorbed into that point, and I could feel myself slipping, slipping into that space. At once it felt like a great vortex as well as a slide; a shimmering spiral as well as an unblinking eye with unspeakable clarity pulling me closer and closer to its mysterious point of oneness. Perhaps my pain and my grief had made my own being more pliable, like a clear, smooth gel. Suddenly, I "heard" words falling like raindrops into the opening that this point had created in my soul.

---

20 Joseph Campbell and Bill D. Moyers, *The Power of Myth* (New York: Anchor Books, 1991), 188.

"Death is necessary." The words were formless, shapeless beings with no letters. The meaning was that much clearer and more poignant. I'd known about death being necessary on some level before this moment, but entering into this realm had awakened every cell of my being much more deeply. The knowledge was no longer confined to my brain or my thought. This "knowing" was so much more than that; I often use an extra "e" to distinguish it from regular knowing: "Knoweing" feels like my head has been painlessly, invisibly hinged and silently opened; pearls of wisdom have been dropped into that space from the vast unknown by the vast unknowing. When they are ripe, these pearls burst open and permeate every fiber, muscle, breath, every heartbeat. I am not the author of this experience, nor do I control it. What is asked of me from this realm is that I say "yes" and that I participate as fully as I am able. The message of this particular pearl was this: Death is necessary. Death. Is. Necessary.

Not long after my son died, I was at one of the centers where I practiced spiritual direction. Our Center was part of a much larger one that could easily accommodate nearly two hundred for overnight retreats. In its gathering space, a nine-by-six-foot Venetian mosaic of the Holy Family had been installed; it was one of the highlights of the building complex and it contained thousands of one-inch square tiles.

I found myself inexplicably drawn to that mosaic in the months following my son's suicide. In a quiet moment, the mosaic would pop into my head. As I walked to the bathroom down the hallway between appointments, its image would follow me, in an almost haunting way. So clearly was it etched into my memory that I had no need to sit in front of it, although there were times when I did that, too. I felt seduced by this intricate piece of art. It had gently yet firmly attached a strong, solid tether to my inner space, and together we began to form some sort of a whole being—the mosaic and me. It was odd, it was surprising, and I found myself welcoming the experience with open arms.

Thousands of tiles drew me, with their voice of clarity and their mesmerizing story that felt like a metaphor for all of life. The voice of that mosaic traveled across the "thin space" and spoke to my being. The beauty of the mosaic conveyed the love with which it was created thousands of miles away in this retreat center in central Connecticut. In one voice, they spoke to me clearly and gently with a tone that could only be described as ethereal:

> *Together, we—the thousands of tiles that are affixed to this wall in front of you—represent the whole of life's experience. Our context can be as personal as your own life experience or as universal as all of life's experience for all of time. For us, life experience includes the span from birth to death. We understand that death is not outside the circle of life; it is intimately a part of it. Each of us tiles represents one moment. When all of us have been attached lovingly and securely to the wall, we form a complete picture. None of us knows the content of each tile. We do know, however, that when complete, we become more than the sum of us. If we say, "No death tiles, we are not talking about death here because it isn't a part of life. It's either a failure or a mistake on someone's part. It's not supposed to happen. Plain and simple," then those of us who are death tiles will fall off the wall, crash to the floor, and break into a thousand pieces. Like Humpty Dumpty, there would be no putting us back together again, no matter how hard you tried. You won't know if you've lost a part of the background, which would leave a hole, but not*

a critical one. In a worst-case scenario, some of the death tiles form the eyes, or part of the smile on the face of baby Jesus, Mary, or Joseph. This loss would be much more visually conspicuous. Either way, we are tiles that work together to form the entire mosaic and we are incomplete without every one of our pieces; each of us is necessary.

The tiles in this majestic mosaic were persistent and unwavering in their truth. With what seemed to be very little effort, they were able to speak to my own battered, weary, broken heart. I wondered often after Matthew's death if only a mother could know the heartbreak of another mother. This mosaic was reinforcing something I'd known before at a much more superficial level: "Death is necessary. Without it, the mosaic—life itself—remains incomplete. Your son's death tile is an important part of this beautiful mosaic, an essential part of its story." Even as I write this part of my story, the enormous and lasting comfort I received from the mosaic seems unlikely, improbable, dubious. Not real. And yet, the consolation from this message remains rooted firmly in my heart. And I've not known my heart to lie or to betray me in matters of this import.

Then there is the story about compost—doesn't get much earthier than that. We live on an acre and a half of rocky hillside that's primarily an oak forest. Our leaf piles are renowned for their size. We have two designated spots that serve as our leaf dumps when we begin the long, seemingly endless task of fall cleanup. One is in a spot we simply call "up in back." Several years ago as I was hauling another tarp-full, I accidentally dug my toe into the pile, which is many years old. Luckily, I didn't fall, just unearthed all this dark, rich, lush earth-like substance. I was stunned. We had followed no special formulas, had done no assiduous babysitting, done nothing to this pile, in fact, other than to dump thousands of leaves there every fall and let them settle.

What my toe found was beyond words. The "compost" had no odor and the texture was something I'd never felt before: crumbly but not dry. The word "black" was woefully inadequate to convey the rich darkness of its color. To my utter surprise, it had no odor. No odor? How could that be? All that rot must have smelled and been disgusting at many points in its transition from a mess of leaves to fertile compost, although there was no evidence of that now that its transformation was complete. It seemed to defy logic. We began using it in all our gardens, with spectacular results. A friend had stopped by during the spring, and couldn't believe it. My sister-in-law, an experienced gardener, was equally impressed. Both wished they could easily appropriate some, although neither had gardens. It was so beautiful it was hard not to want some. I couldn't stop letting it sift through my open fingers. The feel of the material was compelling; it seemed to contain secrets known only to itself. As I was becoming more and more involved with its texture, I felt as if I was also becoming more and more a part of *it*.

And this gorgeous substance is one of the outcomes of death; its transformation seemed easy, the effort minimal. Leaves decomposing through the four seasons we experience here in the northeastern United States. Season after season. Year after year. The natural cycle of life was working its mystery and magic, bringing forth out of death the support necessary for the sustenance of new life. Again the message I continued to need to hear in the aftermath of my son's death. Death. Is. Necessary.

❧ • ☙

Our nineteen-year-old cat, Inky, taught me everything I needed to know about death being "natural." She began to fail in the spring of

2012. She became less active, ate and drank less, slept more. She'd been the queen bee of the family from the moment she entered our lives, a six-and-a-half-pound little ball of soft, black fur whose only desire when she was younger was to be the One in Charge. She became adept at intimidating our eighty-pound lab. As she aged, her primary craving was to curl up in your lap and be cuddled. In this phase of her life, we began to call her the Quintessential Lap Cat.

She waned slowly. Her decline was unquestionable, though our capacity for denial seemed to materialize as fast as her death approached. One of us—usually me—would say from time to time, "You think she'll rebound, don't you?" as I looked for some reassurance from my husband. He would generally say very little in response, leaving me to figure this one out all on my own; he was much more pragmatic about the cat's future. At the same time, we did talk about it and we made a conscious, deliberate, thoughtful decision to let her die naturally. What would or could a vet do? Extend her life by a few days or weeks? At what cost to little Inky? How much additional suffering?

Slowly she stopped eating and drinking completely; the shift was gradual and felt organic to both of us. Nonetheless, it was heartbreaking day after day to look at her water and food bowls and see that neither needed refilling. I longed to pick her up, and I did, once or twice. Even though her limp little body had very little energy, I could feel that my efforts distressed her. She was clear that she did not want to be held. My heart sank into the depths of despair. Some days, the only way I knew she was alive was because I could see her tiny chest rising and falling with each breath. She carved a little death nest underneath my husband's desk, directly across from our sleeper sofa.

Deep down, I knew that my attempts to cuddle her weren't about comforting her; they were about comforting me. I felt some shame around that even as I tried to simply stay with my own desire and understand that my need to be soothed was rooted in my deep love and affection for her and for myself. I tried to reassure myself that it was OK for me to need consolation, too. At the same time, I remained chagrined that it took all my willpower to refrain from touching her or picking her up.

We kept the children informed. They knew she was dying. We knew she was dying. Inky had become a cherished member of our family when they were adolescents, and their love for her equaled our own. We laid out newspapers near Jorg's desk, carefully smoothing them out, as if that would be her miracle cure. We placed a bowl of water and a tiny amount of food near her self-chosen tomb, just in case she should decide to drink or eat. She did neither.

I'd sit across from her on the couch, talking softly to her, hoping that perhaps she'd find my companionship soothing in some way. Again, I knew I was fooling myself. Everything I'd read about animals dying is that Inky was choosing to die in the most natural way mammals die: find a quiet space to be alone and stop eating and drinking.

Father's Day weekend we were scheduled to go on a family camping trip. My hand-wringing had begun long before that. I began to waiver about our decision to let her die at home with no intervention. She seemed to be doing much better with that than I was. So I began to start the conversation all over again, sometimes silently in my head, sometimes out loud when Jorg was home. I was finding it is so very hard to let go.

"Jorg, I think it's time to call the vet. She's dying." It was hard for me to admit that part of me was worried about what people would think. I'd already decided what they would think: that we were *bad* pet owners. Right down to the tips of our toes, we were *bad*. I convinced myself that not a soul on earth would agree with our choice to let her simply go. The children were relatively quiet about our decision, but my imagination even had them agreeing with my evaluation of the situation. At the same time, I couldn't imagine a strange person—even a skilled vet—examining her, poking, prodding, perhaps even putting a needle in her flaccid skin. That seemed the cruelest thing. And yet . . .

"Susie, they can't do anything for her. She's old. She's dying. There isn't anything that will save her." How his no-nonsense attitude disquieted my soul in times like this, although his stance was exactly what I needed. What I *wanted* was to shake him and tell him it was high time he brought out his magic wand to save the day.

I returned to my wretched hand-wringing, second-guessing state of anxiety. Deep down, I knew we were making the right choice. I just couldn't connect to that space inside of me in a way that would provide the assurance and support I needed. I'd sit across from her, simply watching her. We prepared the food for the camping trip. We packed the car. We watered the plants. We made sure all the windows were closed. I was inventing every delay tactic in the book so that we wouldn't have to leave her.

Inky stayed put, silently curled up in her cozy little death nest. Quiet. Occasionally, she'd move her tongue in what I perceived to be a feeble attempt to lick her mouth, and I could hear the dryness of the movement. When I did, I'd kneel on the floor, careful to keep as far away from her as I could, lest I disturb her space, and put one drop of water on the tip of my index finger, hoping she'd take it. Nothing. No interest. She was far more at peace with the way things were going than I was. I was finding absolutely *no* comfort in the way of nature; under my skin, my whole being was chafing and restless, resisting her death with everything I had.

The weekend passed and we returned home. We knew Inky would be dead. We dreaded this moment as much as we were hoping that whatever suffering she had experienced had, indeed, come to an end. Our footsteps up our long path to the door were leaden and slow. She'd found the energy to move her little being from her hiding spot under the desk in the study to the sliding glass doors in the living room. This had always been her favorite place to lie from the time she was a kitten. She was stretched out in the sun, body warmed from the dappled afternoon sunlight that was filtering gently through the oak forest. Her soft, black coat seemed to be absorbing and also radiating the comfort so inherently present in that moment. She died in her little patch of gleaming sunshine in a space that was dear to her. Her loss left an enormous hole in our family, one that we chose not to fill for two years.

Dear, dear Inky died naturally. I believe she died peacefully. I do trust that, hard as it was at times, we honored and were faithful to her process. Her innate wisdom about death far exceeded my own during most of those last few weeks of her life. I knew that and was deeply humbled as well as grateful. She had become one of my great teachers through the way she died—so natural in the animal kingdom, so foreign, such an anathema, seemingly wrong or immoral to many of us more highly evolved creatures. After all, we are supposed to fight, to squeeze every last breath out of our lives, to fear, to resist, to use all means available, to "live" one more day, no matter the suffering, or the cost emotionally, spiritually, physically, or financially. Just. One. More. Day.

The conversation around humans dying naturally has created a furor for many years. It seems to have increased over the past decade or so as individual states have passed various versions of "Death with Dignity" laws allowing patients to choose no treatment or treatment to help a person who is terminally ill die with dignity. A Google search with the words "right to refuse food and water" yielded almost 14 million hits in the summer of 2014. A search using the words, "right to die states" produced 458 million. Compassion & Choices, founded over thirty years ago is, according to their website, "the leading nonprofit organization committed to helping everyone have the best death possible."[21]

The governments of several nations are engaged in a conversation that crosses political, moral, and religious lines. Desmond Tutu and George Carey are two prominent Anglican clergy who are in favor of legislation that would allow doctors to assist patients with less than six months to live to end their lives. An article in *The Economist* states that "traditional religious beliefs seem to play less of a role in shaping public opinion than they used to."[22] At the same time, the article concludes with this somber assessment: "Even countries that accept the principle of assisted suicide will find that the debate is just beginning."

In the U.S., five states have succeeded in passing measures over the past seventeen years: Oregon was the first in 1997; Washington followed in 2008; in 2009, Montana; Vermont in 2013; and in 2014, New Mexico. In my home state, Connecticut, advocates for "Death with Dignity" legislation tried in 2013 and again in 2014 to pass such a law with no success, although it made it further in the process in 2014. An article in *The New York Times* on February 8, 2014, reported that "research in Oregon indicates that for many patients, just knowing the option is there has proved a great comfort . . . Of the 122 patients who obtained lethal drugs in 2013, only 71 used them, the rest dying naturally with

21 "Who We Are," Compassion & Choices, https://www.compassionand choices.org/who-we-are/about/ (accessed January 4, 2016).
22 "Where to Go to Die: In a Small Group of Countries Helping Someone to Die Is Not a Crime," *The Economist* (July 19, 2014), http://www.ecomist.com /news/international/21607888-small-group-countries-helping-someone-die-not-crime-where-go-die (accessed January 4, 2016).

the pills in a drawer."[23]

Archbishop Michael J. Sheehan of Santa Fe weighed in when a district court in his state declared a constitutional right for "a competent, terminally ill patient to choose aid in dying." He explained to legislators there that "the church teaches that life is sacred from conception through to natural death . . . This assisted-suicide thing concerns me . . . I foresee dangerous consequences."[24]

Reading that, I found myself drifting into cynicism. I did not agree with the archbishop, and I found myself wondering how he defined "natural death." I began to doubt that he'd ever seen anyone die on a respirator after failed bypass surgery as my dad had. As I described in Chapter 3, by the time he was pronounced dead by the doctor in charge, every one of his incisions had turned black; his feet had turned a musky blue color and were as cold as food just out of the refrigerator; the smell of rotting flesh was strong and cloying enough to transcend the typical hospital antiseptic odor; and the respirator was still clicking as they began to detach his poor battered body from the miles of tubing that had kept him alive for fifteen days. I was tempted to write the archbishop and tell him this story. The cliff notes version would look like this:

---

23 Erik Eckholm, "'Aid in Dying' Movement Takes Hold in Some States," *The New York Times* (February 8, 2014): A1, http://www.nytimes.com/2014/02/08/us/easing-terminal-patients-path-to-death-legally.html (accessed January 4, 2016).
24 Ibid.

Dear Archbishop Sheehan,

I would like you to help me understand how rot-ting to death on a respirator after failed heart bypass surgery could ever be classified a "natural death"?

Thanking you in advance for the kindness of your reply,
I remain,

Very truly yours,
Susan S. Jorgensen

Following the Connecticut struggle most closely, one of the things I began to wonder was how, even if bills and laws pass, do we begin to affect the underlying attitudes that are so fiery and quick to equate suicide and this movement most frequently referred to as "death with dignity"? Though the legislative piece is proving to be most difficult, my own sense is that the underlying attitudes will be equally if not more challenging to overcome.

Poignant, heart-wrenching stories around death with dignity abound. One that particularly touched my heart involved Armond and Dorothy Rudolph, aged ninety-two and ninety, respectively. Both were suffering from physical ailments and both had been recently diagnosed with an early stage of dementia. They were housed in an assisted living facility in New Mexico. Together, they had decided to stop eating and drinking; this was not the kind of life they wanted to live any longer. After three days of not eating and drinking, they told the staff their plan. The staff called 911 and the facility quickly evicted the couple. Fortunately, they were able to find a private residence, where Armond died ten days after he had begun his fast, and Dorothy died the day after that.

The Rudolphs' son, Neil, launched a campaign entitled, "Peace at Life's End," as his response to his parents' experience. The president of Compassion & Choices, Barbara Coombs Lee, offered this comment at the launch of the campaign: "Stopping eating and drinking is peaceful and painless and people throughout the country don't avail themselves of it. . . ."[25] How did songwriter Laura Nyro know enough, at the age of seventeen, to write, "And all I ask of dyin' is to go naturally"?[26] What if we were able to begin to offer more freely this option to our human loved ones, perhaps with the comfort measures that hospice care makes available? How I long to be able to more openly and freely follow the lead of death—there is so much wisdom in this universal act. How I long to trust its nature as the one and only thing that completes life, that the very essence of life is death, that it is absolutely necessary, that it has a beauty that is as moving and deep as the experience of birth.

Like you, Laura, I only wanna go naturally.

25 *Good Morning America.* "Elderly Couple Refuse Food, Water to Die; Get Evicted from Facility." Written by Mikaela Conley, ABC News, August 18, 2011. http://abcnews.go.com/Health/couple-stops-eating-drinking-end life-son-launches/story?id=14327416 (accessed January 4, 2016).
26 Laura Nyro, "And When I Die," More Than a New Discovery, Verve Folkways, LP. 33 rpm, 1967.

EIGHT

Completion and Beauty

So shall my word be that goes forth from my mouth;
It shall not return to me void,
but shall do my will,
achieving the end for which I sent it.

—Isaiah 55:11 (New American Bible)

This particular Bible verse has had the most influence over me in terms of understanding death as one form of "completion." This is an older translation; it is the only one that I have prayed with and pondered. Other translations are equally beautiful, most frequently substituting the word "empty" for "void"; "accomplishing" for "achieving"; and adding the word "prosper" as a second description that lets us know that the "word" will achieve *and* prosper.

I first encountered this Bible passage during a moment of desperation. I was co-facilitating an eight-week adult enrichment series on the Catholic liturgy. My partner and I had arrived early to set up and in the course of getting the "coffee-and," we discovered a huge oversight.

"So," I asked my partner. "What are you planning to do for Opening Prayer?" This was an important element of our structure as it set the tone for the evening's topic and usually we alternated doing it.

She looked at me wide-eyed, her mouth expressing a mixture of surprise and alarm. "I thought you were doing it tonight."

"Oh, oh. I thought *you* were doing it tonight." I could begin to feel the panic rise. The class was set to begin in fifteen minutes and the early birds would start arriving any minute.

"OK, let's not panic," I said. I refused to let this oversight get to me, though tiny beads of perspiration had begun to collect just above my upper lip and my tongue had started to stick to the roof of my mouth. *Who, me? Anxious?*

Thinking out loud, I continued, "I'm going to do something I've never done before. I'm going to pick up my Bible and simply open it and point." Many people pray this way; some of my directees have had amazing experiences with this method. I've never counted myself among them, however.

I sat down and did just that. And the passage that presented itself was Isaiah 55. In my Bible, some of the chapters in Isaiah have titles; this one was entitled, "Invitation to Grace." In that moment, it felt exactly like that: Grace. An oversight on our parts had brought us a lovely, lyrical passage from the Hebrew Scriptures (Old Testament) that is proclaimed every year during the Roman Catholic celebration of the Easter Vigil ritual. It was a perfect prelude to our evening's focus.

Not long after that, my dad died. I read the entire chapter for his funeral. Seven months later, my mom died. Again, I did the same. I couldn't absorb everything that chapter was conveying to me in those grief-filled weeks and months. However, though I wasn't fully aware of what was happening, I began to realize that this passage had been no "accident" or random event. Isaiah's words and vision became the balm my soul sorely needed, its comfort, its teacher.

Verse 11 affected me the most deeply:

So shall my word be

that goes forth from my mouth.

It shall not return to me void . . .

I began to understand that I was being given glimpses of death, its purpose, and its function; they were different than I'd ever seen. Over time, I began to associate "my word shall not return to me void" with the sense that we do not die until we're complete. Isaiah was helping me weave death and completion into an intricate, unified pattern that was beautiful to behold. I also found the verse that follows this one illuminating; it was part of the work my soul was being asked to consider:

Yes, in joy you shall depart,

in peace you shall be brought back;

Mountains and hills shall break out in song before you,

and all the trees of the countryside shall clap their hands.

—ISAIAH 55:12 (NEW AMERICAN BIBLE)

Joy. Peace. The image of "trees clapping their hands" was a sure expression of celebration. These, too, are three of the experiences that are tucked inside the experience of completion. It brings me great comfort to know that, at the time of my loved ones' passings, the mountains and hills were singing and the trees—*all* of the trees of the countryside—were clapping their hands. These poetic images from this gifted visionary don't rob me of my grief; they make it more possible to feel the grief, to process it, to welcome it as one side of the coin.

A quote by a Tibetan Lama in *My Grandfather's Blessings* supports this idea of completion. He states that we die "not because we are ill but because we are complete."[27]

---

27 Rachel Naomi Remen, *My Grandfather's Blessings: Stories of Strength, Refuge, and Belonging* (New York: Riverhead Books, 2000), 313.

Isaiah 55 reflects this sense of completion in verse 11. While the words "achieve" and "accomplish" are frequently used to translate this verse, I prefer the word "complete," which conveys this aspect of death more fully.

Looking up the word "complete" in the Merriam-Webster online dictionary offers this insight into the word:

> *having all necessary parts: not lacking anything*
> *not limited in any way*
> *not requiring more work: entirely done*

Applying the word "completion" to death seems so helpful. In obituaries, we often describe the deceased person's accomplishments, giving the reader a fuller sense of a person's impact and import in the world. However, accomplishments are tied to linear time and space. This was a very difficult realization for me as I reflected on my grandmother's life. She'd been a good woman in the fullest sense. She was a dedicated nurse who'd worked part time on the maternity floor of a local hospital until she was seventy-eight. She'd lived a simple life, with God as her rock and steadfast presence, and her Bible was always at hand on her bedside table. And she made the best chocolate cake and molasses cookies in the whole world. She died in 1979, a month shy of her eighty-seventh birthday.

By 2014, when the bulk of this book was written, I realized that there were only two people who could remember her well—my brother and me. The factual details of her life were slipping out of human memory; this awareness surprised me and I found myself feeling bereft. Thinking about who would remember her once my brother and I were dead jangled a nerve inside my heart. Pretty soon, I knew there'd be no one to tell her stories. Her "accomplishments"—what she'd done during her lifetime—were mostly forgotten a mere twenty-five years after her passing. I'd saved several pairs of mittens she'd knitted for me when I was in my early twenties—I'd never been able to part with this physical evidence of her presence here on earth.

However, that felt small and insufficient compared to the wise woman I'd known her to be, to the deep impact she'd had on my life. Yes, I was aware that I was carrying part of her into my life, through genetics and through story. As I was sharing my stories about her with my children, I knew that they were listening and remembering as best they could. However, they didn't know her unique aroma of fresh laundry combined with her soap and facial cream—how I loved to hug her for that reason alone. Because they were still babies when she died, they didn't know what it felt like to hold her hand or comb her hair, or how her house smelled when we raced through the french doors of her apartment, into the living room, past the dining room, and straight into the kitchen to see what sweet thing she'd baked for us that morning. The grown-ups overlooked our running indoors, which made the race that much more special.

I knew her storyline itself was growing thinner than a bald man's pate, and sparser, too. The accumulating years were quickly pouring pea-soup fog over the memories. They were becoming less reliable; many had simply been buried by more recent ones. Viewing her life through this lens of accomplishment left me with a hollow feeling that had a sharpness to it. It stung like a surface cut stings until it's been bandaged and is well on its way to healing. I felt little comfort or contentment in that space.

Given the opportunity to look at her death as completion, this new lens became a gift that sustained me. It opened wide the doors of my own inadequate understanding and began to fill me with its wisdom. Grandma died "not lacking anything"; she died when she was "entirely done"; she died only when she had "all the necessary parts." And she died only when she was "not limited in any way." Do I know what those parts were? Or what limits she had transcended as she drew her final breath? No. That was not for me to know. I could speculate with delight that this part of her dying process had brought her into direct contact with angels; this didn't feel like even a small stretch.

The nearly unbearable feeling that the hollowness and temporariness of accomplishment had created in me dissipated completely. Immediately, I felt a lasting comfort that came from the depth and richness of completion. The internal shift I experienced was instantaneous, monumental, shocking. My grandmother had died when she was complete. So will I. And so will you. We will not be lacking in anything; we will be entirely done; we will not be limited in any way.

My own capacity for understanding in this realm, this dimension, this thin space is limited. The very nature of being human is about being limited and the creative ways we improvise to nurture our relationships within these limitations. On some level, it's less challenging to see the completeness of a person's life when they die, like my grandmother did, at a "ripe old age." It was harder when my son died at thirty-four, when he took his own life. I believe that it was simple grace that began to help me recognize my son's death as part of a greater whole, a *much* greater whole. Because of our human limitations, I sense that we're all invited to accept that which we'll never be able to fully see. His death is full of meaning and purpose; it bears, reflects, and affirms the completion of his life. His death also becomes part of what completes the greater whole. Each of our deaths does this. Again, this brings us into a fuller appreciation of how important and critical this second bookend is. We can't ignore it easily or say it isn't what it is without inhibiting the fullness of our lives.

Tension is created when we hold death as a form of completion and an experience of loss. How can death be both? They seem to be in opposition to each other. However, as we become more and more able to hold both, to connect those two circles with intention and understanding, what begins to emerge is the sacred mandorla shape. Brian Jensen describes it thus:

> *The mandorla begins the healing of the split (of the tension of the opposites). The overlap generally is very thin at first, only a sliver of a new moon, but it is a beginning. As time passes, the greater the overlap, the greater and more complete is the healing.*[28]

Let's look at the drawing of the vesica piscis with its mandorla and these two aspects of death as we begin to bring them together until they overlap. They definitely seem to be at odds with each other. How could death be about loss and completion? This reconciliation of opposites lies at the heart of the healing nature of the versica piscis and the mandorla.

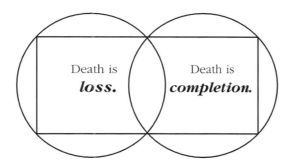

Death is
loss.

Death is
completion.

---

28 Brian Jensen, "Mandorla: Ancient Symbol of Wholeness," *Sandplay: The Sacred Journey* (Spring 1997).

Once we've entered the almond-shaped space of the mandorla, we're in the realm of "both/and," with no experience of time and space. It is wholeness, seamlessness, and One. This space allowed me to embrace the overwhelming loss of my childhood friend, my grandmother, my parents and in-laws, my son, and, more recently, a dear friend. *At the same time*, I embraced death as an expression and experience of completion. There can be no mistaking the healing qualities of this space. My first response was one of release, a great long "Ahhhhh" that came from every part of my being. Body, mind, soul sing this one note that circles, dances, and weaves something new inside and outside of me. I am no longer in a space that feels locked, static, prison-like.

In this realm, I'm also more able to accept that my capacity for knowing has clear boundaries and constraints. A passage from the Bible speaks of these human limits with eloquence and clarity:

> *For my thoughts are not your thoughts,*
> *neither are your ways my ways, declares the Lord.*
> *For as the heavens are higher than the earth,*
> *so are my ways higher than your ways*
> *and my thoughts than your thoughts.*

ISAIAH 55:8–9, ENGLISH STANDARD VERSION

I don't pretend to understand the when and why of my son's death. At some point, I was able to see how much harm it was doing to me to try—and I've been able, through grace, to let go of the need to "get it." I do believe that, at the moment of his death, he had fulfilled his purpose for being here. I do believe that he died at the moment he was complete, and this lens of understanding provides me with comfort and consolation. Julian of Norwich's simple words stirred once again in my heart, "All shall be well, and all shall be well, and all manner of thing shall be well."[29]

29 *Revelations of Divine Love*, which also bears the title *A Revelation of Love—in Sixteen Shewings* (Norwich, England, 1395), Chapter XXVII.

Sandra Maitri, in *The Spiritual Dimension of the Enneagram: Nine Faces of the Soul,* expresses this timeless thought six hundred years later:

> *. . . Cataclysms and natural disasters only seem not to be part of God's Will if we take a subjective position about them and decide that they are not good things. Human behavior that is hurtful, insensitive, and negative may seem bad to us, but it is nonetheless emanating out of the souls whose ultimate nature is Being, even if they are not functioning in harmony with It. So their actions, too, can only be part of God's Will. Additionally, it is a huge presumption to decide that an event is bad and should not be occurring, since if we could see the bigger picture that encompasses the future (Here I would add "the past" as well because our memories are incomplete and tend to distort.), we might see that the event actually has a beneficial function in the long run—and that long run might be well beyond our lifetimes.*[30]

I don't see it as a stretch to include our experiences of death in the meaning of the word "event," which appears in the fourth sentence. It's then possible to see how Maitri's words apply to our conversation about death and augments our understanding of it.

❧ • ☙

The last of this quartet of characteristics of death from this side of the coin is that death is "beautiful." A number of years ago, the elderly mother of my dear friend, Margaret, died at home. Mrs. Callahan was an elegant woman. I didn't know her very well, although at one point my friend had asked me to go with her to visit her mom, who lived about two hours from us. I jumped at the chance and knew what a

---

30 Sandra Maitri, *The Spiritual Dimension of the Enneagram: Nine Faces of the Soul* (New York: Jeremy P. Tarcher/Putnam, 2000), 157.

privilege it would be to share a meal and conversation with this woman I so admired.

We had lunch with Mrs. Callahan in her home, which was right next door to the home where she'd lived for most of her adult life and had raised her four children. She invited me to dig up some of her lily of the valley to take home; they've thrived in my own garden and now greet me every spring with a part of Mrs. Callahan's soul. The fullness of her well-lived life, her strength, and her dignity nod to me as clearly as the tiny white bell-shaped flowers bob in the cool spring air. Their lovely aroma enters my being and before I know it, Mrs. Callahan and I are having an intimate, wordless conversation in my garden.

Several weeks before she died, I went to visit her. By then, she'd moved into Margaret's traditional house on a tree-lined, quintessentially New England street, and hospice had assumed her care. A hospital bed had been brought into my friend's lovely living room. Mrs. Callahan's nurses and aides were calm, thoughtful, unobtrusive women who understood death, and even more surprisingly, seemed to understand each family member's needs around the process. It was uncanny to be around them.

I walked into the house, warmly greeted my friend, and then turned into the living room. I noticed my breath and it surprised me—it felt jagged, like it was skimming over some unseen, sharp, and barbed tines of apprehension. I was finding something challenging in being that close to death, even though I hadn't anticipated anything huge or extraordinary. The hospital bed was startling; perhaps that accounted for my anxiety, although it wasn't the first time I'd seen one in someone's home. Still, it seemed so big, so out of place amidst the furniture; the soft, plush carpeting; and the well-appointed draperies. And Mrs. Calahan seemed so very small in the middle of it, as though the bedding itself, freshly crisp and brilliantly white, had already begun to absorb her dying body.

I went to the side of the bed and gently picked up her veined hand, its skin semi-transparent and fragile-looking. "Mrs. Callahan, it's Susan Jorgensen, one of Margaret's friends." Her eyes were closed and I spoke softly so as not to disturb her. I don't remember if I said more than that or whether she responded.

After staying for what felt like the right amount of time, I became aware that I was having a hard time letting go of her hand and saying goodbye. I felt rooted to the floor, bound firmly in place by some unseen force. What was going on, I wondered. In the moment, I reasoned that my difficulty in leaving was because I knew I'd never see her again. Though I hadn't known her well, I had great respect for her and had loved her as the mother of my dear friend. I continued my internal rational explanation—that the finality of this moment had caught me by surprise, left me feeling slightly off balance. That was all this was.

It wasn't until many years later that I realized that my reluctance to leave was about much more than saying a final goodbye to a magnificent woman. Once again, the realization happened in a conversation of considerable depth with a friend. I'd started telling her the story of Mrs. Callahan and how hard it had been to say goodbye and leave her bedside, that it hadn't made much sense to me at the time. I told her with a bit of embarrassment how I'd rationalized my experience and conveniently forgotten about it—until this very moment. That my time with Mrs. Callahan would surface now felt carefully orchestrated and not of my doing; something greater was at work here and I smiled a little.

In the presence of my friend's steadfast, unwavering listening and in her interest in my story, slowly it began to dawn on me that, when I'd turned to go into the living room and approach her bed, I'd also walked through a portal of some sort, not visible to the human eye. Finding words for what had happened during our time together was one of the more difficult tasks I'd faced in quite a while. No wonder I'd forgotten about it. I was stumbling, throwing out words toward my friend like random balls in a pitching practice, taking most of them back because they didn't fit, keeping a paltry few.

My friend was undeterred, committed to her listening, asking more questions to help me really notice what had happened between Mrs. Callahan and me that day. At first nothing I said seemed even a little bit accurate—one of the more common indicators that signal to us that we're in this other realm. In graduate school, I'd learned that the official term for the phenomenon is "ineffability," which means "too great, powerful, beautiful to be described or expressed." My friend's loving presence helped me to persevere; eventually words began to come that felt like they fit.

The portal was softly arched, wide, with thick broad walls that had been delicately spun of gossamer threads. It could have been, too, that this portal had been carved from the clouds and transported through the heavens, brought down close so that this next part of her journey would be neither arduous nor long. It could have been both.

Mrs. Callahan had entered that Celtic thin space, the other realm. Unbeknownst to me, I'd entered that space, too. At the time of our visit, I'd been focused solely on two things: my own slight discomfort and my desire to be careful with her because she seemed so fragile and I didn't want to inadvertently hurt her. My intense focus had caused me to miss the fact that her soul had graciously invited me in and my soul had graciously accepted. Reflecting back on our time together, I became aware that my own human heart and soul had quaked and trembled as I approached her bed.

The mysterious beauty of this nuanced space gently pierced, opened, and bid me enter. It was humbling to be invited to be there with her; the word, "beautiful" pales when I apply it to the experience itself. The beauty had so many layers and facets, a precious and extraordinary diamond of the soul. I was aware of a peace infused in everything and everyone; it didn't matter that I didn't know what "everything" or who "everyone" was. I "saw" angels in diaphanous dress whose wings became a sacred instrument accompanying the heartbeat of the universe, hushed and rhythmic. A mantle of tenderness wrapped around me as it sunk deep into the core of my being. I "heard" a unique silence that had its own unspoken, unsung sound. It was then that I knew why it was so hard to leave the beauty of that space with her. I "knew" in that mysterious way of "knoweing" that only the soul has, that I was experiencing one of the stages of her death with her and it was, indeed, elegant.

Thank you, Mrs. Callahan, for revealing to me how beautiful death is.

NINE

Words

As I ponder the power of the word to incite and divide, to calm and connect, or to create and effect change, I am ever more cautious in what I say and how I listen to the words around me.

—SUSAN SMALLEY[31]

Words galvanize us. They become a rallying point for causes. They become the force that cheers us on just when we think we can't take one more step and we're only a hundred steps from the finish line. It doesn't matter that we're among the last, the contingent that we could rightly name "the stragglers." Someone along the race route will shout out enthusiastically, "You can do it, just a little further. Keep up the good work." And those words become an invisible motor under our sweat-soaked running shoes that propel us over the finish line, victorious, proud, triumphant. A stranger's words hollered at just the right moment can be as important to us as a presidential commendation. Having speed-walked a half-marathon in 2001, I can still feel the power of the words that people used to encourage me. And they are priceless.

---

31 Susan Smalley, "The Power of Words," *The Huffington Post*, March 28, 2008, http://www.huffingtonpost.com/susan-smalley/the-power-of-words_b_81918.html (accessed January 5, 2016).

Words also become the knife that cuts without compassion or fore-thought, delivering hurt feelings, wounded pride, damaged self-image and self-esteem. Remember the childhood chant, "Sticks and stones may break my bones, but names can never hurt me"? As children we repeated this mantra because words had hurt us. We used this chant to convince ourselves otherwise.

When we were kids, my brother and I were more verbal than phys-ical fighters—we used words to taunt each other until one of us had reduced the other to tears. We'd both perfected and honed our tech-nique and it didn't take long for either of us to get the desired result. I remember us saying to each other, once the crying had begun, as if the verbal insults had not been enough, "The truth hurts, doesn't it? The truth hurts." Such is the nature of words to mock, jeer, ridicule, goad.

Because words *and* names change our sense of who we are and what we might become, examining their impact on us is critical. In junior high, my classmates decided to name me "Fatty." My self-image was irrevocably altered in that one moment and this two-year-long taunt by my peers never completely healed. On the other hand, names also carry waves of positive energy with them—life changing in the opposite way.

Seven months after I was diagnosed with lung cancer, my doctor ordered oxygen. On their own, my lungs could not sustain a saturation level of greater than 90 percent most of the time (normal is 95 to 100 percent). So began my first experience with the world of DME—Du-rable Medical Equipment. I received a tank of pure oxygen in case of power outages. I got an O_2 converter that sat on my dining room floor with fifty feet of tubing. I was literally tethered to the physical world now, in a helpful way. And I had a portable machine that gave me about two hours of concentrated oxygen for my outings.

During one of the first weeks I was on oxygen, I met my husband at a local restaurant. On the way there, my little machine sat in the passenger seat next to me; I had carefully buckled him in—no seat belt violations for this babe and her companion. I was deep in thought, considering how this ten-pound machine was bringing me much-needed comfort and mobility. It didn't seem right that he should sit there *nameless*; he needed a proper name so that we could have proper conversations and expressions of gratitude. On the one hand, these seemed to be the most normal ideas I could be having at that moment; on the other, I feared that I had begun to see a few cracks beginning to appear in the frame of my sanity.

I let those go and just let my imagination run. It didn't take long for my DME to tell me its name—it required no effort on my part. Thus was "Buddy" christened in my car as I chuckled through the remaining miles to the restaurant. My husband arrived at almost the same time I did and, fortuitously, we got parking spots right next to each other.

He greeted me with a big smile as I was unbuckling Buddy and setting him on the ground. "I've been thinking," he said.

"Yea? About what?" My attention at that moment was completely absorbed in making sure Buddy was ready to roll safely into the restaurant while my delicate nostrils remained in one piece; my learning curve and I were becoming best friends.

"I think you need to name your machine," he said, nodding. He seemed proud of his suggestion. The light in his face expressed it all.

I threw my head back as far as I could and laughed out loud. "I just *did* that!" I exclaimed. "Let me introduce the two of you: Buddy, meet Jorg. Jorg, meet Buddy." We could not have shared a sweeter moment of laughter. From that moment on, I tried always to introduce him. Not only did "Buddy" get a name, my younger daughter decided he needed eyes so he could see where he was going. She found the best googly eyes and sewed them on his case, creating a face for him. I looked for opportunities to introduce him when I was in public, especially to children so that they wouldn't be afraid of this weird woman with tubes coming out of her nose.

What did this naming do? I'm convinced that the act of naming is very important. Karen Sternheimer describes it this way: "When we are known and not anonymous, we are more likely to behave in ways that reflect positively on our identities."[32] Those of us with terminal illnesses are faced with greater and greater levels of dependency and equipment to help us live well; they are one of the sources of comfort measures that the dying *need*. And they can be the proverbial pain in the-you-know-what. We can growl at them, resent them, hate them even; what remains is the fact that they'll usually be with us for the rest of our days. We can choose to face them negatively, or we can find ways to "play," to reflect positively, as Sternheimer suggests. We can also adopt the "both/and" approach that invites us to find ways to honestly speak of the two sides—the resentment or the gratitude, depending on the moment, our mood, or the situation. In so doing, we avail ourselves of the miracle that is the sacred space of the mandorla.

In the cancer world, we speak these words: survivor, fight, battle, crusade, war, struggle, beat, defeat, lose, win. In the death world, we don't have that many words because we avoid or truncate conversations that would help us develop other common phrases and words. We can

---

32 Karen Sternheimer, "The Importance of Knowing Names," *Everyday Sociology Blog,* January 17, 2014, http://www.everydaysociologyblog. com/2014/01/the-importance-of-knowing-names.html (accessed January 5, 2016).

talk about death as failure of someone or something, as an event to fight vigorously or triumph over. We bestow praise on dying patients who endure treatments that sometimes cause great suffering and pain, motivated by extending their lives by months. Often, we're puzzled and secretly wonder about those who say "no" to medical regimens for their disease. At least, this has been my experience. Our words are limited and insufficient.

I've often proclaimed that I received far more from my directees than they have ever received from me—an observation from my own heart-space that was both humbled and filled with gratitude in their presence. I learned a lot about the power of words from one of my directees whose sister lived in the town next to hers. As children, they'd been close, best friends even. As they aged, they grew apart. A family feud involving multiple relatives and money issues arose when they were in their mid-forties. My directee kept bringing the story into our sessions, focusing on the negative attributes she saw in her sister. As far as Emily was concerned, Patty couldn't do anything right. She was bossy, selfish, lazy, *and* narrow-minded—for Emily, that trait had to be the worst. Patty didn't like anybody. No wonder her husband had divorced her and she was estranged from two of her three children. Emily was emphatic and convinced of the rightness of her assessment.

This went on for several years. I would listen, ask questions, invite her to pray about her relationship with her sister, ask her where her sense of God was as she was struggling so tenaciously. It was clear to me that, beneath her angry rhetoric, Emily was suffering. She was missing her sister and didn't know how to get out of this enormous hole that her negative words had so efficiently and neatly dug. Jack Schafer, a professor and retired behavioral analyst, would call this phenomenon "negative primacy." I referred to it in sessions as a frame that wasn't always helpful. I was also aware that I was finding her "stuck-ness" somewhat frustrating.

One day she came to our appointment and she was more excited than she'd been in many months.

"I've had a huge shift in my awareness." She could barely contain her enthusiasm and her face was wreathed in a smile that seemed big-ger than she was.

"So, tell me; you've certainly grabbed my attention," I said enthusi-astically. I could feel my heart beat with an anticipation that filled me with delight as I leaned in a little closer.

"I was thinking about Patty *again*. All negative *again*. And then I realized that this is all I ever do. I say disparaging things about Patty all the time."

I nodded in agreement. "I know. Your relationship with your sister has been really hard for you these past few years." I wanted my voice to express the compassion and understanding of my heart and I didn't want to convey any of the frustration I had been feeling.

"Well, I've been a broken record!" She exclaimed. "I don't have to talk about her that way anymore. I realize that if all I use are negative words to talk about her, that's all I'll see. She's so much more than that." She stopped for a breath because her garrulous words had come out like a newly thawed spring river gushing and splashing over its banks. Her normally sallow complexion had taken on a rosy glow.

"That's quite the realization, Emily." I was trying to take it all in because I knew intuitively that this was a *huge* shift.

"I know!" She agreed and continued, "I'd forgotten how funny Patty is, how much we enjoyed each other's company, how good she is with detail stuff—I'm lousy at it—and she's such a good cook. I'd also for-gotten how we used to sit down on Friday afternoons and plan special

Sunday dinners we'd share with our families." She was simply brimming over and her enthusiasm was contagious. I could almost see a visible connection being rewoven between her heart and the love she'd always had for her sister. It would take time for the connection to strengthen, but Emily had taken the first and most important step and I had no doubt that it would continue.

"I'm going to stop with the negative words," she declared. "They're not helping." And at that, her eyes filled with tears and I reached for the box of tissues.

This experience was as life-changing for me as it was for her. I began to look at words as frames. We have hundreds of experiences in any given day: I walk across a busy city street. This is an experience that can't change, no matter what I do. What I can change is the frame I put around it: I can choose one that's either negative, positive, or neutral. Consider the world of art. Imagine that I have an exquisite unframed painting. If I choose a mat and frame that either overwhelm the art or clash with it, the art suffers; it may even get lost completely until all you can see is the frame. If I choose a mat and frame that enhance it, the piece grows in beauty. It practically pops out of its carefully chosen home. Same piece of art, completely different effect, depending on how I choose to frame it.

Emily discovered this in her relationship with her sister. Her negative words had effectively built an ugly frame around her sister, obscuring an important piece of her sister in the process. The negative was so powerful that it had distorted many aspects of their personalities and relationship. Emily had begun to forget the good times that had been part of their life together for many years. As she began to reclaim positive language, she found that her sister was still her sister, complete with *all* her annoying qualities; the feud was still the feud.

However, much to her surprise and delight, Patty's endearing qualities began to reappear, to sparkle again.

Not long after Emily had her "aha" moment, I had the opportunity to meet Patty. Without realizing it, Emily's words had helped me create quite the haggish image of Patty. In my mind's eye, she was a dumpy woman with a sharp chin, thin hair, a nasally voice, and small, darting eyes that always looked slightly suspicious. Imagine my surprise when in front of me stood a petite woman with dark curly hair, one dimple, and a gentle laugh. I chuckled to myself and just shook my head. Ah, the power of words to create frames that influence how we hold our stories and experiences.

Susan Smalley observes this about words:

> *Verbal insults, verbal abuse, and the power of words to affect your emotions and actions are well demonstrated in science. For example, scientists have found that just hearing sentences about elderly people led research subjects to walk more slowly. In other research, individuals (who) read words of "loving kindness" showed increases in self-compassion, improved mood, and reduced anxiety.*[33]

Ever since I was diagnosed with breast cancer in December 2005, I've been much more aware of the words we use around cancer and death. A colleague had asked my permission to have my name put on a t-shirt for a 5K walk/run to raise money for cancer. I was honored and said, "Of course you may. Thank you for thinking of me." The solicitation that was sent to potential contributors was worded like this (emphasis mine):

---

33 Susan Smalley, "The Power of Words," *The Huffington Post*, March 28, 2008, http://www.huffingtonpost.com/susan-smalley/the-power-of-words_b_81918.html (accessed January 5, 2016).

*This is a chance to add names to the Honor Shirt in celebration of cancer survivors, support of those still **fighting their battle** or in memory for those who **lost their lives** to cancer.*

I was saddened by these words, struck particularly by the stance they conveyed of fighting, battle, and the phrase "lost their lives." In this context, the word "death" is the immediate, though unmentioned, event, camouflaged by the phrase "lost their lives." I attended a day-long conference with spiritual activist and teacher Stephen Jenkinson a number of years ago; he had strong opinions about using the word "lose" to reference death. I became an advocate of his position. I didn't need to be provoked to take out my soapbox any time the opportunity presented itself to rail about the effect of the word "lose" on the experience of death and dying.

I'd start my little speech by saying that I wasn't sure I knew what it means to "lose your life." I can and often have lost my keys, my train of thought, my way. I've lost money, games, clothing. But lose my life? It's not the same. Merriam-Webster online lists these three as the top meanings for the word, "lose":

> *to be unable to find (something or someone)*
> *to fail to win (a game, contest, etc.)*
> *to fail to keep or hold (something wanted or valued)*

If I have "lost my life," isn't there some sort of implication that I, or someone else, would galvanize into action to help me find it or get it back? I'd work very hard to find my keys, get that wayward thought back, find a better map for my next adventure, look in every drawer and coat pocket for my money, call every friend I know to see if I'd left my coat in *their* closet, and I'd figure out why I'd lost that game so I could win next time. But my life? These methods to "find" it don't work in this situation. Dead is just that—dead. And if I'm dead, it's not because I've *lost a battle* or failed in some grave and catastrophic way. My doctors haven't failed. My family and friends haven't failed. I'm dead simply because it was my time to die; my life would be complete at that exact moment.

The August 4, 2014, issue of *People Magazine* featured Bindi Irwin on its cover; the title was, "Bindi Irwin on Her Dad: 'It's Like Losing a Piece of Your Heart'"[34]; the article had been written to mark Bindi's sixteenth birthday. The article quotes Bindi, "I remember after we lost Dad . . ." Her father, Steve Irwin, was the famous crocodile hunter who had died tragically in 2006 following a freak attack by a stingray. The article gave me pause and it helped me to step off my "lose" soapbox.

I looked up the word again and discovered that the dictionary *does* define "lose" in terms of death as their fourth of eleven definitions: "to suffer loss through the death or removal of or final separation from (a person)."

I began to think that the word itself softens the finality of death, perhaps makes talking about it a little easier. I wondered if using the word "lose" in reference to death could be another example of both/ and. Sometimes it *does* feel like we've "lost" our loved ones; they don't show up for dinner, they don't take out the trash, they don't go on hikes with us. Where have they gone? In one sense, we *have* lost them. "Losing" can convey a less harsh condition, a state of impermanence that we sometimes need, even if just for a little while, until we, our souls, and our hearts are ready for the deeper truth.

34 Michelle Tauber, "Bindi Irwin on Her Dad: It's Like Losing a Piece of Your Heart," *People* (August 4, 2014), http://www.people.com/article/bindi irwin-remembers-her-dad-steve-irwin (accessed January 5, 2016).

But there are more words to talk about death. For me, the invitation is clear: to intentionally begin to use these other words. For those who do not believe that anything happens after we physically die, the simple word "die" works fine. To indicate afterlife, though, we might say *passed, passing over, crossed the threshold, transitioned from this life to the next.* They sound awkward because we don't use them very often. And words like *dead, transitioned, passed,* and *crossed over* convey a clearer sense of permanence.

How might the image of this mandorla be conveyed? What would we name as its foundational energy? I would call it the tension of permanence and impermanence:

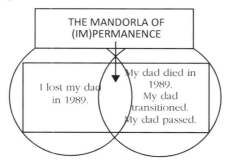

Remember that t-shirt and the framework of war that it conveyed? Diagnosed with a terminal illness, dying day by day, did I want the primary invitation and instruction to be to "fight the battle"? Frankly, I didn't have the energy. This framework felt limiting and negative, especially if it was the only one I had at my disposal. Psychologist Jack Schafer remarked, "Words cannot change reality, but they can change how people perceive reality. Words create filters through which people view the world around them. A single word can make the difference between liking a person and disliking that person."[35] In this case, a single word can make the difference between more easily understanding and accepting death, and completely resisting and rejecting it.

35 Jack Schafer, "Words Have Power," *Psychology Today* (November 2, 2010).

With that in mind, what if we changed the wording of that t-shirt solicitation and removed the references of violence and war (fight and battle) and references to death as "losing"?

Original Wording:	*New Wording:*
"This is a chance to add names to the Honor Shirt in celebration of cancer survivors, support of those still fighting their battle or in memory for those who lost their lives to cancer."	*"This is a chance to add names to the Honor Shirt in celebration of those recovering from cancer, support of those still undergoing treatment, or remember those who have died from cancer."*

And herein lies the rub: this second wording lacks the cry of battle that rallies us effectively. It doesn't read as passionately; it lacks the pizzazz of the first version. We've created a successful fund-raising culture around these words of war. Fund-raising around breast cancer brings in an estimated—and very impressive—$6 billion yearly.[36] We are bred to respond to the battle cry; this semi-automatic response to perceived and real threats has protected us and kept us safe through centuries of aggression.

We're conditioned in such a way that our only response must be to fight until we reach the bitter end, to *never, ever* give up. Following this path, those who choose to fight become our inspiration, our celebrated heroes and heroines. But I believe these words and the stance they require exact a toll, not only in the world of cancer but in the wider world of all medical conditions that lead to death. As Jack Schafer and Susan Smalley, a behavioral geneticist, writer, and activist, have so

---

36 Lea Goldman, "The Big Business of Breast Cancer" *Marie Claire*, September 24, 2011).

astutely noted, words have power. We become what we speak and hear. Violence begets violence. It's finally time to take the risk of expanding our language around terminal illness and death.

For a time, I worked with some alternative medicine treatments after I was diagnosed with terminal lung cancer. My practitioner and the woman who referred me to him told me that I had to believe that I'd be cured or the treatments wouldn't be as effective. This felt like a thinly veiled threat to me. I was clear with both of them: I didn't believe this, nor did I have the desire to believe it. My focus and intent were about staying connected to the flow of divine energy, to my life's path. Too many times during the course of my adulthood, I'd ignored my gut's wisdom in favor of what *I* wanted or thought *I* needed. Almost always, those choices caused a separation between this divine flow and my soul; the experience created angst and *agida* deep within me. Everything felt out of sync; nothing fit. I'd lost my balance and grounding.

So, if I was meant to be cured and live, then that was what my heart sought; if I was meant to die from this cancer, then that was what my heart sought. I'd been blessed with a single-minded heart whose focus was on being connected to God in all ways and always; that gift brought me great comfort. One of my new words became "cooperating" with the Source of All, God, the One, Allah, Great Spirit, Being, Yahweh, the Universe, Presence, Divine Energy. *And.* Cooperating with Death when my discernment and counsel of others led me to do so. I was clear that I didn't want to go to war, fight, or win a battle. My soul was intent on pursuing one thing: to cooperate with the Magnificent Mystery who is the Source from which I came and the One to whom I will return.

A *New York Times* article caught my attention.[37] It read:

> In October 2012, for the first time, Komen featured a woman with Stage 4 disease in its awareness-month ads, but the wording carefully emphasized the positive: "Although, to-day, she has tumors in her bones, her liver and her lungs, Bridget still has hope" [my emphasis].

I applaud the team that approved this ad. They surmounted our prevailing culture's phobia around dying. But it took them thirty years to risk featuring a dying woman in an ad. Imagine the positive impact this must have had on other women dying with metastatic breast cancer, other women who were dying just like Bridget was. Suddenly, they were no longer pariahs and outcasts but people who were worthy of note by the Komen Foundation.

On the other hand, I was immediately curious about what they defined as Bridget's "hope." Here's another example of the power of words. "Hope" when metastatic breast cancer has spread to a person's bones, liver, and lungs? What does that kind of "hope" look like? I could offer a guess here and say that they meant there was hope for a cure, implying that we should donate sooner rather than later. The writer informed her readers that Bridget died in April 2013, six months after the Komen ad had run. I found a photo of her on the Internet; she was twenty-nine when she died. I couldn't stop looking at her face; her radiance; her large, dark, clear eyes. I've learned more about her since reading this article. On the surface of things, I would have thought our energies would be in opposition. Over thirty years of lived experience separated us; she chose treatment until she died while I rejected it. But

---

37 Peggy Orenstein, "Our Feel Good War on Breast Cancer," *New York Times Magazine*, April 25, 2013.

her eyes told me that we had a lot in common, especially our passion for life, no matter how we interpreted and manifested it.

But I still wonder how truthful the Komen ad was. How realistic? How real? I've also been struck by the cheeriness that some breast cancer patients seem to have. A celebrity who'd been recently diagnosed with breast cancer was being interviewed on television. When asked how she was feeling, she didn't skip a beat and with quite a bit of enthusiasm exclaimed, "Great! Just great!" More than anything, I think people with terminal illnesses deserve truth, and the space to be real to the degree that they're able to hear and grasp it.

We need to expand our vocabulary so we can talk more fluently about how we feel when we're diagnosed with terminal illness. I'm sick. I'm tired. I'm scared. I'm *dying*. Sometimes people would call me and ask me how I was doing. Often my mind was a blank, and in those times I would say simply, "Well, I'm dying." I did worry that my honesty felt like rude bluntness, that it was offensive. Most of the time, the words aren't complicated or hard. There may be days when a dying person is feeling great; I suspect there are also many days when they're not feeling great. We need space to express all our feelings so that we can receive the support we need and deserve.

Back to "hope" for a moment. I came across this quote about hope:

> *Hope can be a powerful force. Maybe there's no actual magic in it, but when you know what you hope for most and hold it like a light within you, you can make things happen, almost like magic.*[38]

Whether you are the dying person or family or friend, it can be helpful to articulate your own hopes through the process. It may take

[38] Laini Taylor, *Daughter of Smoke & Bone* (London: Hodder & Stoughton Ltd., 2011), 288.

courage to talk about your hopes; it may take courage to hear your dying loved one talk about his or her hopes. But I think our hopes give us courage—yet another "both/and." Your hopes may surprise you and they may change as your dying time draws near. I do believe that hope is "like a light within" and, as Taylor says, the thing you hope for most will help you make things happen.

For me, I'm hoping for many things; a physical cure isn't on my list, but that's just me. Some of my hopes may be unrealistic; many are not. I'm hoping to live vibrantly and fully until my body can no longer support that. Then I'm hoping my spirit will carry on until my body dies. I'm hoping for death with dignity. I'm hoping that my loved ones find the comfort, solace, and support they need in the days, weeks, and months leading up to and then following my death. I'm hoping that my death isn't too painful on any level. I'm hoping that my connection to the Divine remains strong, clear, unwavering. I'm hoping to be fully conscious until the end. I'm hoping to finish this book.

The Power of Words. *Die. Dead. Death. Pass Over. Cross the Threshold. Transition. Cooperate. Hope. Courage. Practice.* Above all, *Practice.* To become comfortable and adept with these emerging ways to tell our stories about dying and death, we must practice. Our stories will, letter by letter, word by word, become more honest and more real. The more new words we use, the more we'll find. We may find that some don't work; that's when appreciating the "learning curve" can come in handy.

One day, we may discover that we, too, can declare, "Today is a good day to die." While this has traditionally been understood to reflect a Native American's stance on the day of battle, one Native American and Vietnam War veteran has been able to expand on that conventional meaning. After his own harrowing experiences during the war and then, many years later, three close encounters with death, Lee Standing Bear Moore wrote:

> *I steadfastly hold the ways of the Beauty Path in my heart and thus fear of death is insignificant. The depth and breadth of Indian philosophy and spiritual belief has always served me well in times of crisis. Just as the water of life is not distressed by its many changes, from liquid to solid to vapor in the eternal circle, I am not afraid of my body changing into spirit. After all, the same water that appeared at the time of Creation remains on earth today. The idea that my spirit will one day join with those of my ancestors and other loved ones is an appealing thought.* [39]

Let us be inspired by Lee Standing Bear. Let us remember, honor, thank, and mourn all who have died—our ancestors stand ready and waiting to brightly illuminate the bookend of death that we are all eventually given. It can be that simple; it can be that nonviolent. Let us all work toward a language around terminal illness and death that reflect its qualities of being necessary, natural, complete, and beautiful.

---

39 Lee Standing Bear Moore, "Today Is a Good Day to Die," http://www.manataka.org/page1909.html (accessed January 6, 2016).

TEN

Conversations

Conversation should be like juggling; up go the balls and plates,
up and over, in and out, good solid objects that glitter in the foot-
lights and fall with a bang if you miss them.

~ Evelyn Waugh[40]

Being diagnosed twice with cancer forced the specter of my death for everyone who knew and loved me. With my first diagnosis, I learned that cancer and death seemed to mean the same thing for many people. If you have cancer, then you might as well start writing your obituary. And if you have cancer, then I could have it, too. And I could die. That's how the mostly unconscious reasoning goes. Even though we believe that we have made progress in terms of dispelling the fear and anxiety that surround the diagnosis, I've encountered many people who still can't say the word cancer out loud. Instead, they start bravely, "I heard about . . . (a long, weighted pause, followed by) . . . your illness." We're so scared of cancer because it feels that death can't be far behind.

---

40 Evelyn Waugh, *Brideshead Revisited: The Sacred and Profane Memories of Captain Charles Ryder* (New York: Little, Brown and Company, 2012).

I responded to their fears, hoping that my voice would relay the comfort I was trying to convey in the face of their trepidation, "You mean my cancer?" In my quieter, saner moments, I wanted to remove at least part of the stigma from the disease. I wanted to provide openings for folks to talk about cancer, about dying, about being dead. Maybe if I wasn't afraid to talk about it, I could encourage them not to be so afraid either. One friend wrote me one note on loose-leaf paper telling me how sorry she was about my "illness." She left it on my desk at work. I'd have been just as happy taking her by the shoulders, shaking her, thrusting my nose into her face, and demanding, "Say it, would you please? Cancer! Cancer! Cancer!" But later, reflecting on my own strong reaction, I realized I was not only frustrated with her and our culture; I was angrier than I wanted to admit, even to myself, that I'd gotten this dreaded disease.

I heard many things pertaining to what people had imagined was my imminent death—some interesting, some enigmatic, some just plain dumb. At one point, I was tempted to write them all down, and then I said to myself, "Whatever for? What would be the point?" Something saved me from that very bad idea. I discovered that most folks couldn't use the word "death." They were caught up in discovering the causes of my cancers. Was it radon in the basement? Electric lines? Diet? Lack of exercise? Tap water? Microwave? Pollution? Implied, I think, was that once they figured out the mistake I'd made, they could avoid the terrifying knock of the Grim Reaper at their door. Susan Kuner, one of the authors of *Speak the Language of Healing*, dispelled all those negative dead ends in a single paragraph:

> *Vegetarians and yoga teachers die of breast cancer, as do meat eaters and tap water drinkers. Breast cancer finds confident*

women as readily as it does those who are meek. Tumors come
to both the sunny and the depressed.[41]

If somehow I were cured, then they would be that much safer from the disease themselves. If I died, the threat to them would become all the more real. I was rapidly discovering that fear doesn't need to be founded on any sort of logical reasoning. Fear just *is*. I found conversations around death more difficult to traverse, more painful, more frightening in some ways than the challenges my breast or my lung cancer themselves presented.

After the first few numbing months following my breast cancer diagnosis, I began to glimpse what I needed: someone to give *me* an opening to talk about dying, to talk about being dead. I didn't want to make nice—I couldn't, really. I needed someone to ask me how I was doing and then settle in to listen to me answer the question, no matter how long it took. When I was diagnosed with terminal lung cancer eight years later, I knew more clearly what the soul work was that was begging at my door. My need was more pressing because I was beginning to feel the constraints of linear time. Someone had flipped the sand timer without so much as a nod from me. I began to pursue more honest conversation as I became less afraid of hurting other people's feelings and sensibilities.

One night, I began a conversation with my husband. We'd already gone to bed and turned out the lights. How come it's easier to start a conversation of this weight and import when it's dark and quiet, when the earth has dialed down its energy and the atmosphere has an almost pregnant feel? Naked, spooning, breathing restfully, I began.

---

41 Susan Kuner, *Speak the Language of Healing: Living with Breast Cancer Without Going to War* (Berkeley, CA: Conari Press, 1999), 30.

"You know, I'm probably not going to wait for my body to die. I think my body will be able to just go on and on, even without extraordinary measures to keep it alive. However, I doubt I'll have much quality of life at all. When I become diapered, drooling, no matter how lovingly cared for, I think it will be time. I don't want to live like that— counting the days, waiting, experiencing false alarms. I don't want you to have to care for me like that, either, day after day."

I paused. I'd chosen my words carefully, rehearsed this conversation many times in my head. Somehow, speaking it silently in my head, it sounded better. As I heard my words fill the space around us, they seemed woefully inadequate, a size XXL shirt on a size XS body. They simply didn't work; they stretched and stretched and couldn't begin to reach the sentiment I was trying to express.

My husband interrupted my internal dismay, "It's your body, Susie. It's your decision. You can decide whatever you want." I couldn't figure out the emotions underneath his response and this unsettled me further.

I uttered my protest quietly. "No, you don't understand. I want you to be a part of the decision."

I felt him energetically wanting to pull out of this conversation. It was late. He was tired. I was tired. We were both tired. Of a whole lot of things—my cancer being at the top of that list at the moment. He repeated himself, "You have to decide that, Susie. I can't decide that for you. It's not my decision to make." I sensed his frustration and his impatience; it would be hard to miss at this point and my dismay deepened.

"No. It's *our* decision. Please listen." He shifted a little, picking up my building desperation. To my relief, I sensed that he'd returned to the conversation, and I was relieved. "I want *us* to decide. I don't want to decide this by myself. It wouldn't be right."

"So what do you want exactly?" In the dark, I wasn't sure what he was feeling at this moment, but his voice seemed tighter to me, edging into the murky emotional territory of exasperation. Perhaps this conversation wasn't such a good idea after all, even with all my careful planning, thought, and practice.

"Well, I want to come to the decision *together*. I want to say to you, 'OK, I think it's time now. I love you too much to want you—or the girls—to suffer watching me suffer. It's time. Out of love.' And then, I want you to say to me, 'It's time. I love you too much to watch you suffer one moment longer.'"

I could feel my own passion rise now like a full moon in winter; I had broken through the bonds of my own uncertainty and sense of failure. The words had come and they fit and they felt lovely in my mouth as I spoke them; now they felt like music, not sour notes as I heard them flow softly over my parted lips. I also felt my dearest husband listening deeply. An important shift had happened.

"I get it now. And we'll just do this together." He is a man of few words, and he spoke these from his heart. A hug passed between our nestled bodies and we drifted off to sleep.

A few evenings later, we picked up this critical conversation thread. I didn't feel I'd said everything that I needed to say. We were in our same positions as our first conversation, quietly nesting, our long legs entwined, the darkness of the night holding us both tenderly.

"So, remember our conversation about both of us choosing the right time for me to die? I just want to say a few more things."

Because he was a man of few words, I have found other ways to know that he is listening—it is a non-verbal felt sense. He snuggled in a little deeper, and said, "OK."

"Well, it's about the context of our decision. It seems this very important choice is one that our *relationship* makes. Do you understand what I'm trying to say?"

"Sort of."

"I know; it's hard to talk about this stuff. It's like there are no words for it." I wanted to ease into this and I also wanted to share what limited understanding I have, because it *is* limited. Again, I found myself stretching for words, like trying to reach a can on the highest shelf in the kitchen and finding it *just* out of reach. One more little ounce of effort, a bounce on my toes with hand extended and there they were. The words came tumbling out, inspiring and guiding the conversation that followed. Yet another encounter with the mystery of grace.

"We love each other; we've loved each other for more than forty years. It's not like we're fused and need each other to feel complete, 'cause we're not and we don't. We're far too independent. And yet, in this relationship, we are both more than we are when we're by ourselves and it just seems in keeping with the natural essence of things that choosing the right moment for me to die is about our relationship. Not just about me. Not just about you. So far so good?"

"Yeah, I get that part."

"So it's like the relationship is its own entity, and the relationship is about love, and the relationship makes the choice out of the years and years of the deep, deep love we have for each other. That's it."

"I get it. I understand."

The conversation was providing us with a new context for all that would come: it reflected a more fleshed out, real sense of union and oneness that we already had and for which we hadn't yet found words. I came to a greater appreciation of how well good conversations help us embrace the real, the mystical, the unseen that our souls so easily see. Knowing that the holy was finished for now, the night delivered us mercifully into the mysterious plain of sleep and dreams.

And this was part of the new territory we were learning to navigate. Perhaps there wasn't something new each day, but often there was. We were both becoming familiar with the death bookend; like new parents, we were learning by doing, we made mistakes, but we were equally committed to seeing it through with dignity and grace. We had begun tentatively to use the expression "learning curve." It gentled many situations and provided us with the space we needed to make corrections as they were necessary without turning our relationship into a battleground to air old wounds and create new ones.

Several weeks later, I began another conversation. "You know, I've never died before. This is a whole new ball game."

Jorg nodded his head, "Yeah, I know. Duh."

"Come to think of it, I've never been on oxygen before, either. I was annoyed the other day when you left the power cord to my oxygen concentrator at home. It was *so* not helpful." I was expanding the conversation (carefully and sensitively, I hoped) because I wanted him to know that this particular oversight was pretty inconvenient for me without raising his defenses.

"I know," he answered and I could hear an awareness and recognition in his voice.

"You know, it wasn't a big deal, and yet, it was—leaving the power cord at home meant that I only had two hours of air for a four-hour afternoon. The math really didn't work and I had to leave before I finished my work." I continued, more confident that he wouldn't dismiss my words and I wouldn't offend him. In other words, the conversation felt productive.

So I continued, "Well, we're bound to make mistakes. A lot of them. I think we should just keep talking out loud about the learning curve we're both on when we do. That way, we're not blaming anybody, we're using our energy to figure out how to do things better, you know?" I could feel myself already warming to the expression and seeing how helpful it is going to be.

"Sounds good to me," he agreed, and it felt like we'd not only had yet another conversation about death, but we'd also found a peaceable, workable solution for the many times we were going to screw it up.

Other conversations also happened in this previously unexplored territory of death. I was grateful for all of them, as awkward as many of them seemed at first. Negotiating the awkwardness was like standing on one side of a five-hundred-yard ravine and just being told, "Now leap." No safety net, rope, or line—just thrust yourself naked into the wild blue. One of the first of these conversations was with a dear friend who, at the end of one of our visits, asked, "I hope you'll give me something of yours to remember you by after you go."

"After I go?" Wow. I was stunned. At that point, my cancer was progressing slowly; even though I was clearly in an advanced stage, I still saw myself in "decent" shape. I didn't think I was in that much denial. First impression—could she be any bolder or more insensitive? Drop a bombshell on me just like that with no air-raid siren to warn me? My fourteen-year-old self wanted to duck and cover, but there was no time to do that. Failing that, she needed to spoon out the old attitudes about death she'd inherited and held as absolute truth for at least fifty years. "It simply isn't right to ask me something like that; in fact, it's really wrong and you should know better. Shame on you. Didn't your mother teach you *anything?*" That's what part of me wanted to say. Thankfully, I was able to hold that part of me in check.

Perhaps it was the sincerity of my friend, her honesty, her love for me and mine for her, the deep sharing we'd blessed each other with for many years. Perhaps it was my own newer convictions about death that had been growing since my diagnosis of breast cancer. Whatever was moving in my soul at that moment, it calmed down the impulsive fourteen year old who was seriously offended by her friend's request. Once again, wisdom prevailed. I breathed and smiled, perhaps not my seventy-five-watt smile, but still a smile. And I said, "Of course. What a lovely idea. Thanks for asking."

Later on I found myself thinking about the funeral of my friend, Aelred. He'd been a devoted, committed, passionate Roman Catholic monk. Formerly a Benedictine, he'd more recently professed private vows to the bishop of his diocese. After the funeral, which he'd planned down to the tiniest detail (we'd all joked with him about his control issues from time to time), we went back to his little hermitage for our final gathering. During that time, one of his friends quietly began to pass out little mementos, items that Aelred had carefully chosen to give each of us in his memory. He'd selected a shallow pottery bowl for me, one he had bought in England when he was an adolescent—the one he'd used to mix his calligraphy ink. As a fellow calligrapher, he'd shared the story of this bowl with me, knowing that I'd deeply appreciate that he was giving me a treasured part of himself. It remains a cherished part of my own art studio to this day. My friend's request suddenly became a more intimate request that reflected our own deep bond of friendship.

Second conversation with a dear friend. Equally important. Equally awkward. Ann and I have known each other since we were nineteen. We met pledging the same sorority and we've stayed in contact all these years—we'd held each other's babies, cried at our weddings and mourned the losses of our parents, and vacationed together with masses of children in tow.

She and her husband visited us in the winter of 2014, four months after my lung cancer diagnosis. We have similar taste in clothing. I don't buy lots of stuff; I tend to buy good, timeless pieces, and hang on to them for a long time. We went down to my closet and I began showing her things I thought she might like. She was enthusiastic, and, much to my delight, was doing all the appropriate "oohing and aahing." I've always admired her fashion sense, always said she could make a paper bag look good. Me, on the other hand . . . We were genuinely having fun.

Three or four skirts, several silk blouses, and a couple of jackets and blazers later, we were done. Everything tucked back into my closet. She was looking expectantly at me and I was looking back at her, bewildered. Now what? While we weren't shifting from foot to foot, it felt like we were. We didn't know what came next. She clearly had something on her mind, and I was clearly finished with what I'd wanted to do. What else could there be?

So, she said—and it *was* awkward, "Well, good, then! This is great. But . . . well . . . um. . . ." Her voice trailed off and she was looking away; mutual confusion had stolen the intimacy needed for eye contact. This polished, professionally competent woman was at a loss as to how to ask this next important thing. She was definitely not finished with our little clothing survey. She started again, "How will anyone know that these are the clothes you want to give to me?" The unspoken phrase here was, "after you die."

This time, I wasn't offended or put off; I must have been getting used to these awkward and unfamiliar conversations that stick in our mouths like peanut butter that's sat too long in the back of the refrigerator. I hadn't thought of that. And the solution, at least in my mind, was so simple. "Oh, Annie, I'll put them in a bag, and I am going to write your name in *big* letters on the bag. How's that?"

Again, another five-hundred-yard ravine had presented itself— and we were able to navigate it, if not easily, then with some modicum of grace and satisfaction.

Another important conversation happened with my younger daughter, Stacy, who was twenty-five at the time. All of us had begun to talk a little more freely about death after my breast cancer diagnosis. This conversation was about my obituary. Even though my cancer wasn't terminal, it gave us a reason to broach the topic of death a little more openly and freely, less hampered by cultural and social stigmas.

We'd just been reading an article about a celebrity who'd died of breast cancer and made general remarks about how much we didn't like the way the writer said that she'd "lost her life after battling cancer." I made Stacy promise, should I die of breast cancer, that she'd never allow these words to go to press: "Susan Jorgensen, after fighting her battle for seven years, lost her life to cancer." If she did, I jokingly said, I'd come back to haunt her. (A friend suggested that I tell her that I'd make the Ghost of Christmas Past look more benign than Snow White if she ever penned those words.) Stacy got it because she had a similar objection to the words "fighting my battle" and "losing my life."

A serious conversation? It was, and it wasn't. When we brought up the subject, we both felt an invisible catch in the air that caused a subtle, involuntary change to the rhythm of our breath. However, by the time I'd put on my drama queen voice to demonstrate my vociferous protests, we were equally amused; this was good for both of us.

"Don't you dare even *think* about writing something like that about me," I said as my mock tirade had reached its hysterical peak and I was in full form.

She responded, with an equally mock seriousness, "Never, Mama, never. I promise."

We hugged; we laughed; we kissed. Through our laughter we both knew we'd covered several important points, touched on topics often considered *verboten*. We'd introduced the reality of my eventual death from whatever cause. The second, and perhaps more important point was that, by talking about obituaries, we'd broken through an impenetrable barrier that emphatically said it was wrong to talk about death. We had, in fact, talked about it and nothing bad had happened to either of us. The sky didn't cave in, the ground didn't tremble, no lightning bolts flew down from the heavens. Our conversation gave me hope that we wouldn't feel the need to hide our conversations about dying and death from other family members, as my dad and I had felt that need when he was dying.

But not all conversations went that easily. I was at a small gathering of my women friends in the summer of 2014. My doctor had just put me on oxygen 24/7 because my body alone couldn't sustain a saturation rate of even 90 percent. I got together with these women regularly. It had been one of those quintessentially gorgeous summer evenings where the weather was pitch perfect, allowing us to gather on the hostess's deck overlooking a small, babbling brook. Everything was so perfectly appointed, I felt like were we part of a movie set. All we needed was Jay Gatsby strolling by to complete the scene.

When I arrived, there was a bit of awkwardness. Not everyone knew that I'd "graduated" to oxygen, and I'd debated letting everyone know ahead of time that I had. I'd gone back and forth about it for several weeks. This was one of my regular procrastination tools—if I talked it to death inside my head and waited long enough, I wouldn't have to make any decision. The result was that no conversation did take place ahead of time and everyone had to make her own internal adjustments on the spot to this clearly visual decline in my health. I sensed I'd missed an opportunity to have a conversation that would've helped everyone.

After we moved inside, when everyone had gone out to the kitchen to help themselves to dessert, one of my friends plopped herself down next to me. I was waiting to catch my breath because the simple effort of moving inside the house had taken more breath than I had at my disposal, even with the help of the oxygen. Out of the blue, she asked me, "Are you afraid of dying?"

I was stunned by her question. It felt like such a non-sequitur. Momentarily, I was speechless and then I answered clearly, "No, I'm not." I didn't even have anything to offer to her by way of further explanation. I'd looked at this aspect of death so many times and I'd questioned myself relentlessly about my lack of fear. I wanted to make sure I wasn't just fooling myself. My conclusion was that my lack of fear had strong, tenacious roots and wasn't hiding any delusions. So her question was something I couldn't answer in a short conversation that seemed to be happening on the fly. I also wanted to understand her motivation for pursuing this question. Fear and death *are* big topics. Any explorations in this setting couldn't possibly honor our process or give it the justice it deserved. That said, I was also grateful that she'd waited until we could have this conversation one-on-one and not as part of the entire ensemble gathered to celebrate this lovely summer evening.

Apparently, she wasn't satisfied with my brief response. She asked again, with a probing tone, "Really? You're not afraid?"

"I'm not. Honest. I don't know what else to say." I shrugged my shoulders, at a loss for words. This was one of the odder conversations I could remember having. I figured the strangeness stemmed from my sense that it had originated out of thin air and lacked roots and context. At that point, she got up and joined the others in the kitchen. I was left to catch my breath and ponder our short exchange. I'd long considered myself an advocate for conversations that would help us begin to articulate the complex issues that arise around the experience of death. This was, after all, my impetus for writing this book. Several days later I concluded that there was a time and a place for everything. The timing of any conversation, especially one that explores the delicate and intimate nature of death, was as critical as the conversation itself. Another part of the learning curve.

ELEVEN

Compassion

Compassion: that sometimes fatal capacity for feeling what it is like to live inside another's skin and for knowing that there can never really be peace and joy for any until there is peace and joy finally for all.

~ FREDERICK BUECHNER[42]

My relationship with compassion had a ragged start. At the time, I was busy giving weekend retreats based on the knitting book I'd co-authored with a colleague, *Knitting into the Mystery: A Guide to the Shawl Knitting Ministry.* Most retreat facilities require a photo and a write-up for the catalogue months in advance. Proud of myself because I'd managed to squelch my procrastinator self, I'd sent mine in on time, without a second helpful nudge.

The catalogue came in the mail one day, probably two months before the retreat was scheduled. I turned to the page where the knitting retreat was featured and nearly had a heart attack standing in my kitchen. The retreat was entitled, "Knitting into Compassion." The description talked about how the facilitator would lead the retreatants through a series of presentations designed to help them experience

---

42 Frederick Buechner, *The Alphabet of Grace* (New York: Harper & Row, 1989), 75.

compassion and guide them to a greater understanding of the practice.

I immediately called up the retreat director. "Distraught" was a mild form of what I was feeling. I was stumbling over my words, aghast, speechless, numb, and panicked.

"Jodi, wherever did this write-up come from? This isn't what I submitted. Honest. What the heck happened?"

Bottom line: She didn't know. She checked. The conundrum did not resolve itself and it actually wouldn't have mattered if even Buddha or Jesus themselves had come up with a sensible explanation. The retreat description was in the hands of their entire mailing list. What? Maybe three or four thousand people? It was a well-known, highly respected retreat center with a large following. What was in the brochure was what the retreatants reasonably had a right to expect they would get when they arrived.

Thus began my harrowing countdown. What I knew about compassion would fit into a thimble. My thoughts on the subject were pathetically thinner than gauze and far less substantial. Well, I thought to myself, I'd better get going. First stop: Amazon. I ordered a few books, one of which has become a beloved staple in my library: *Compassion: Listening to the Cries of the World* by Christina Feldman. To say that the book changed my life is, to risk using an oft-repeated expression, quite the understatement. What I had initially perceived as one of the greatest mishaps in my recent professional history became one of its greatest, most valuable gifts. So many experiences in my life work this way that it's become hard to view anything that happens as a mistake, a coincidence, or an accident.

I developed a weekend format that led retreatants through a relatively intense exploration of compassion. I soon discovered that people had many misconceptions about the process of compassion. Some were convinced that compassion meant that you had to forgive or condone the actions of whoever had aggrieved you. Others understood compassion to be the same as "pity," which they viewed distastefully as feeling sorry for someone: a smarmy, superficial emotion that few found attractive. Still others believed that compassion meant you had to agree with the person with whom you were struggling. By the time the weekend was over, many people's conceptions of compassion had changed, some dramatically. My initial lament and panic over the content change became a soft bubble of delight in my heart.

As I prepared for that retreat, I thought a lot about what compassion meant to me, and I realized that one of the most important things I learned about compassion I learned from my older daughter, Amy. A phrase she often resorted to during her high school years was, "You don't understand!" She usually uttered it to me when she realized that my "no" really meant "no." I think she was hoping to "guilt" me into letting her have her way.

"No, you may not go to the all-night party. I don't care if the entire town is going."

"No, you may not wear that skirt to school. It looks more like a Band-Aid than a piece of clothing. Now go put on something a little more modest."

I was so puzzled when she accused me of not understanding. I understood. I had no doubt about that. I considered myself a "with-it" mom, as moms go. How many adolescent girls wouldn't want to stay out all night with their friends? How many adolescent girls wouldn't want to wear the latest fashion to school? Years later, I told her that I figured she probably put the short skirt into her purse and changed in the bathroom at school. We had a good laugh over that one.

After thinking about it for a long time, I finally got it. I realized that I *did* understand. I simply didn't *agree*. The energy of those two stances was completely different. Puzzle solved—and I'd caught a glimpse of one of the important aspects of compassion: understanding does not equal agreement.

Another understanding about compassion came from a situation with a group of women for whom I'd facilitated a knitting retreat. When they learned about my breast cancer, they decided to knit me a shawl of healing and create a scrapbook for me that told the story of its making. Because they lived in many states, they had to mail the shawl from one person to the next. Each person got to pick the yarn she wanted; it became a "Joseph's coat of many colors." Each knitter took a photograph of herself holding the shawl in her home and put it in the book.

When the shawl and book arrived, I was sick from the chemo treatments. I had no energy to absorb their amazing gift. I put the shawl and the book back in the box, leaned it up against our piano in the dining room, and said to it and to myself, "I'll send out my thank you to each of them later." A week went by. Two weeks. Soon several months had passed. "Later" had stretched into a long, tortuous time for me. I was burdened by the guilt I felt for not replying properly to this heartfelt expression of love they had sent to me. I discovered that I didn't have the energy to absorb all that love, or the energy to write all those thank-you notes. One day, the voice that dwells in the other realm spoke to me with love and compassion, something I hadn't been feeling toward myself in a long while. "You don't have to like this." I was beyond stunned. I didn't have to like the fact that I hadn't thanked them, that I had no energy to receive their love?

The chambers of my heart extended a warm welcome to that simple statement. It brought me a much-needed sense of freedom and understanding. It had never *once* occurred to me that "I didn't have to like this." The effect on me was similar to the effect of the "I don't have to agree with such and such" statement. It changed everything. It changed nothing. I didn't get up immediately and put pen to paper to write them each a note. What it helped me to do was to be gentler with myself. By choosing to be compassionate with myself, I was choosing (thank you, Robert Frost) to walk my personal "road less traveled," and it has made all the difference. Initially less than a muddy footpath, it is now two tire tracks in the dirt. It may never become a superhighway, but I haven't lost hope that it could become that one day. Kindness toward self. Grace helped me choose and embrace this novel and initially foreign practice.

My idea of compassion involves exercising a mature understanding for a situation or person; that doesn't mean we have to agree with or condone what happened or what that person may or may not have done—or what *you* may or may not have done. This is more about the willingness to listen with a fiercely open heart to another's story for the sake of learning from others, not finding fault with them. To do this, you may have to lay your own wounds aside for just this moment. I *know* this is *not* easy most of the time. In fact, it may be the hardest thing you ever do.

The other important part of the process is about feeling sorry *with* rather than *for* a person, be it yourself or someone else. Placing yourself *with* another is about embracing and exercising empathy, about giving your assent to walk a mile in another's shoes. Feeling your pain, feeling the other's pain, whatever the situation calls for.

Not long after that first retreat on compassion, I was asked to address the annual gathering for cancer "survivors" at one of our local cancer centers. I didn't hesitate, and I didn't need to search and research what I'd talk about. Compassion seemed the obvious and most appropriate choice. It appeared to me that what we needed, especially around death and/or a diagnosis of terminal illness, was compassion—compassion for ourselves as patients, compassion for ourselves as medical professionals, compassion for ourselves as family and friends, compassion for the disease. These words, from Christina Feldman's *Compassion: Listening to the Cries of the World*, seemed particularly fitting:

> *A friend was diagnosed with terminal pancreatic cancer and was told she had only six months to live . . . the six months passed, and fifteen months later she was still alive, becoming more and more skeletal and weak. I asked her what was keeping her holding so tenaciously to a life that had become torture. She told me she wanted to die well, that she had done so much in her life that was wrong, and this last act of dying was one she wanted to do "right." When I asked her what it meant to die "right," she said she had to die without any fear or regret . . . . Her sister remarked, "She is only willing to die if she can die a saint." The burden of sainthood is a heavy one when our personal ideology equates sainthood with a perfection that denies your humanness. Compassion is made difficult when perfection is demanded.* [43]

My story around this issue is similar. When I started the chemotherapy treatments for my breast cancer, I was determined to go through the eighteen weeks without any drugs to counter the side effects. I would be tough. I bravely threw down my gauntlet: "Superwoman, are you ready to meet your match?" It was a strong chemo and

43 Christina Feldman, *Compassion: Listening to the Cries of the World* (New York: Rodmell Press, 2005), 84–85.

when it was time for my second round, I was still plagued by the side effects from the first. That was not supposed to happen according to *my* plan. My version of sainthood included boundless energy and an indefatigable presence of being. I went to my oncologist eating humble pie all the way and said, "Give me everything you've got for these side effects." So much for my high ideals about how I'd get through chemo. So much for my warped sense of and need for perfection.

Where does the practice of compassion begin when either we or a loved one is facing death? Within our own hearts. I've discovered four attitudes that hamper our ability to be compassionate with ourselves. There may be more, but these are the ones I've been working with to deepen my own practice of self-compassion:

❖ When we think we *should* be feeling or choosing differently than we are;

❖ When we *want* to be feeling or choosing differently than we are;

❖ When our friends and family think we *should* be feeling or choosing differently than we are;

❖ When our friends and family *want* us to be feeling or choosing differently than we are.

Remember that lovely shawl those women had sent me? I desperately *wanted* to be different, to dash off those thank-you notes lickety-split. But I couldn't, and I was mad at myself, beating myself up every chance I could. This was definitely *not* helping the situation. It wasn't giving me more energy, it wasn't helping me to love or understand myself. Quite the opposite. In terms of family and friends, if I sounded discouraged or talked about how badly I was feeling, they'd sometimes tell me things were going to be fine, I was going to be fine, not to worry. I knew they meant well; I knew all their responses to me came from a place of love and their own desire that I not die soon, if ever. However, rather than encourage me, often their words felt *discouraging*. Rather than opening up the conversation, they closed it down. I longed to have them say as compassion filled the space between us, "Of course this is hard. Would it help to talk about it some more right now?" Ah . . . a much-needed opening would appear into which we could enter and have a heartfelt conversation.

My dream slowly evolved into creating an environment that would allow me to develop and sustain a compassionate stance. The bellicose words that predominated the cancer world contained little tolerance for this type of conversation. Likewise, if I was busy worrying about my own and everyone else's "shoulds" and "wants," I was creating a stranglehold on what was real and true for me.

The more I rejected the words of war, the more my connection to my cancer cells changed. They were victims, too. I sensed that they were sad, they were sorry, they didn't know how this had come to be, they didn't want or like their condition any more than I or my doctors wanted or liked them. The longer I sat with this sense, the more my broken cells began to feel like a bunch of two year olds who were seriously out of control and wanted more than anything to have someone impose the control they couldn't.

To my surprise and relief, I experienced compassion in this new place, both toward my cancer and toward my body. A different world filled with other possibilities began to emerge from my confusion. Gone were the "shoulds and wants" that I'd imposed upon myself. This newfound kindness made me strong enough to let go of my family's and friends' "shoulds and wants" when to me they seemed neither true nor helpful. From within this new place, I could engage in an interior dialogue. At last, I could talk with my body about all that was happening. My body's cancer cells ceased to be invaders, enemies, something that meant to kill me, fiercely, completely, and irrevocably. Instead, they became unwilling, powerless participants in an encounter with terminal illness.

What did I say to my body? "I am so sorry that you have to go through this." By the time I started chemotherapy, I was able to declare, "I am sorry that you—the whole of you, not just those out-of-control cancer cells—are being poisoned. I am sorry that it has to be this way."

Likewise, my body could reply, "I know; thank you for letting me know how you feel," as it soaked up the comfort that I was directing toward it.

It was the same with my breast. As I prepared for my mastectomy, I was able to genuinely and freely lament, "I am going to miss you so much. I wish there were another way." Lovingly I could speak those words as I stood in the shower the morning of my surgery, carefully and sadly washing it with antiseptic lotion. For the very last time. Really? Hard to comprehend that I would never touch this breast again. How *had* this come to pass? I didn't want to turn off the water; I wanted to stay in there forever; I couldn't face what lay ahead for me. Every moment of that shower was filled with an equal mixture of loss and agony: loss for this body part that had been a part of me for so long; agony because I knew that *today* I would wake up from surgery with a jagged eleven-inch-long incision, stitches, and drains. This was definitely *not* a fair exchange.

While I was on retreat six months after my mastectomy, I was able to write this letter in my journal to my breast:

I want to tell you, wherever you are, that I miss you. I am sorry that I complained incessantly about how big you were. Women are never satisfied with the size of their breasts—they are either too big or too small. Go figure. I am sorry your cells went crazy and started making unhealthy tissue that would have eventually crowded out and eaten all the healthy tissue. I am sorry for your pain. I am sorry for your sorrow. I am really sorry we couldn't give you a proper burial. You were a part of me. It's so strange to think of you as tissue on a slide or as medical waste. Hazardous, probably. You could never be medical waste; you were an important part of me. I don't regret donating you to medical research and yet, it seems so unnatural that we couldn't bury you in the earth and lovingly return you to the universe. Somehow, the circle of life is completed when we can feel the weight of the damp soil and the wood of the shovel handle, rough and coarse in my hands. I am so sorry.

And, with the strength of sorrow empowering it, I discovered that my cancer felt free to speak to me.

I am sorry that I am so out of control. It is not my intent to be this toxic, this lethal. Everything feels like such a mess right now. I'm scared, too.

The whole of my body—the healthy part as well as my beleaguered breast—could feel the energies of kindness and sorrow simultaneously. Another mandorla was beginning to make its home in my soul. I imagined that the cancer was grateful to find words to express itself. Being able to enter this sacred space had the same effect on me as if someone had offered me a drink of water after I'd been wandering the desert for weeks with nothing save the clothes on my back. The relief was palpable and unambiguous; my flaccid, lifeless heart had begun to beat again. The language of compassion and this newfound gift of dialogue brought me a sense of wellbeing and wholeness that transcended any healing that medical treatment was able to bring about.

Many parts of the terminal illness/dying/death experience clamor for compassion: the spaces where we're afraid of dying, of upsetting our family and friends, of how much treatment will cost. Then there are the spaces where we're angry: angry that our bodies have betrayed us by getting sick or angry at ourselves because we haven't taken care of them well enough; angry at God or at how our friends have responded or not responded; angry that our lives have been so dramatically altered, our bodies diminished, our glorious plans and hopes for our futures so shattered by our imminent deaths. Finally, there are the spaces that make us sad, where we just don't know who we are anymore because our illnesses have left us weak, carved us up, made us impotent, hairless, foggy, or numb.

When our souls are invited to fill our voices with compassion, what we will hear is, "It's OK to be scared. It's OK to be angry. It's OK to be sad. It's even OK to be depressed within limits. You're OK. You. Are. OK. It's OK to be—yup—*imperfect*." This kindness will help us take essential steps toward understanding and acceptance. This gentleness will assuage the need to medicate or pathologize perfectly normal responses to perfectly awful situations.

Many people who are affected by our terminal illness/dying/death experience also clamor for compassion. There are days when they may be just as scared, angry, sad, or depressed as we are. They may not want to talk about "it." They may not want *you* to talk about "it." I had a conversation with a colleague, Georgia, while I was going through chemotherapy for my breast cancer. She was distraught. Georgia told me the story about her friend who'd gone through cancer and chemotherapy. Trying to be supportive and helpful, Georgia had responded by telling her about someone she knew who had gone through the same thing. Georgia had offered what she thought were good suggestions on getting through it. The gist of her advice was, "Be grateful for all the people who are helping you. And I know you are going to learn something from all of this. I just know you will."

Georgia looked at me with her bright blue eyes filled with sorrowful incredulity. She was near tears as she told me that her friend had gotten mad at her and walked away. "What did I do wrong?" She pleaded with me. I sighed. I could see what she had done—she hadn't stayed with her friend's story. She hadn't given her friend enough time and space to really talk about her pain and suffering; she had deflected it. It can be much easier to talk about someone who is not in the room, easier to talk about something that happened in the distant past. I prayed for compassion. For her and for me. I'd had so many thoughtless comments thrown my way by then that I was running out of patience for the well-intentioned stupid things that fall out of people's mouths. I knew I needed to be careful.

"Georgia, I know you were trying to be helpful." I spoke thoughtfully as I drew in a deep breath, silently praying not to make the situation worse by saying more stupid things. I knew I was perfectly capable of doing so.

"Susan, I was. You know me well enough to know I would never hurt anyone intentionally."

"I do. And sometimes the simplest responses are the best." Believe what I am telling her, I said to myself: keep this simple.

"Like what?" she asked.

"Well, tell her that what she is going through must be very hard. Find as many ways to say that one sentence as you can. See how she responds. Keep her talking about her experience."

"Really?" she didn't quite trust me. "I figured it would be better if we didn't talk about it, you know?"

"She trusts you, Georgia. If she didn't, she would never have started the conversation. My hunch is that she just needs to talk and talk." I paused to let this sink in.

"So just tell her this must be hard, very hard? That's it?"

I nod. "You can also tell her how sorry you are that she has to go through this. Again, find as many ways as you can to say this to her. My hunch is that she is being brave for everyone else she knows—all her friends and her family. She doesn't feel she has to do that with you; what an honor, Georgia."

Georgia narrowed her eyes as she looked at me and she also started moving her head up and down as well as back and forth. It was a perfect physical expression of two conflicting ideas: I believe you and I don't. "I never would have thought of it that way, Susan. Thank you."

Practicing compassion is hard work. Often I've wanted to walk away from a thoughtless or hurtful comment in anger and condemnation, full of disbelief that anyone could be that stupid. One of my favorites was the one that Georgia offered her friend: "You'll learn something from this; I know you will." The angry part of me wants to sneer and snarl, "What if I don't? Then what?" At that moment, there is not one compassionate molecule in my entire being. Not one. Then the challenge becomes, "OK. Take a deep breath. Can I be compassionate with myself in this place where I'm this angry?"

My other favorite has been spoken by friends who mean well, who are kind-hearted, smart, humorous. And they do love me—I don't doubt this for one second. I might be lamenting about how someone's thoughtless comment has hurt me. They will respond sincerely and with heartfelt intention, "They are only telling you this because they love you, Susan."

"Grrrr." My barking response is waking up and I am so tempted to get snarky; too many people have reminded me that people have said thoughtless things to me because they *love* me. What I want and desperately need is for them to be compassionate with *me*. Just for a little while. I don't want them to be compassionate with *them*. I want to be selfish right now and completely claim their compassion for myself. I want their outpourings of kindness to be the arms that hold *my* raw and throbbing heart, the hands that take my own in theirs. I want them to feel bad that I have been the recipient of a thoughtless comment that has hurt me. If I am overreacting, I want them to be honest about that—that's what friends are for—but not until they've commiserated with me, walked in my shoes of indignation and hurt, and reached out to sooth my aching soul.

The practice of compassion is about discovering that place in us where we can say, "Our family and friends are scared, too. We're all scared. Dying and death are scary. Wouldn't it be good to just acknowledge this instead of turning it into the elephant in the middle of the room that no one can talk about?" We need to find the ability to be honest with each other. The openness to tell and to really hear the good, the bad, and the ugly of our journeys with death are made so much easier when we are able to practice compassion. This practice gives us the freedom to be where we are and allow others to be where they are. This stance leads us out of the prison of recrimination and criticism and brings us straight into the richly textured spaciousness of non-judgment. No right. No wrong. Just "is-ness." For me, this is a gift that cannot be measured; it truly is a breath of much-needed fresh air in a space that we have kept locked up for far too long.

Not long after I was diagnosed with terminal lung cancer, one of my best friends stopped by for a cup of tea. We've known each other for more than thirty years; ours is a deep relationship where we can only be honest. As she was leaving, she gave me one of her hallmark big hugs as the tears were running down her cheeks. "I am going to miss you so much when you're not here any more."

I hugged her back fiercely. "I know. This is *so* hard. I can't imagine not seeing you, either." Honest. Refreshing. Real. This is the sweet fruit that compassion bears, the nourishing salve that coated both of our hearts and filled all the fissures that my impending death had created.

Finally, compassion leads us to that place where we can consider those who tirelessly care for us—our doctors, our nurses, the office staff that field our many phone calls, the technicians that conduct our tests. Where our health is concerned, we need the system to be perfect, seamless. It is not. We need the system to work with efficiency and timeliness. It does not. There are few things that are more broken in America right now than our health care system. My sense is that we all suffer alike—patients, families, doctors, and nurses—and we have few places to express our suffering. We don't have to like the brokenness, especially when it compromises our own wellbeing. We don't have to settle or agree with the system. The gift of compassion is the ability to really know that, to walk in each other's shoes, to imagine each other's challenges, to reach out to one another with increased patience, understanding, truth, and, above all, love. Could there be a better starting point for change?

Let me close this chapter with more words from Christina Feldman:

Compassion is not just a feeling; it is a response to pain that is deeply rooted in wisdom . . . compassion can rescue us from despair and blame and allow us to live with dignity and integrity. Ultimately, it can bring to an end the most painful separation between self and other. Compassion is sometimes defined as "the heart that trembles in response to pain."[44]

---

44 Ibid., 14–15.

TWELVE

Business

. . . if health becomes a business, if a patient is a client, that's the end of medicine.

—DR. GINO STRADA[45]

I was diagnosed with Stage II B, triple negative breast cancer in December 2005. Having had four previous stereotactic biopsies to examine suspicious areas of microcalcifications, my diagnosis didn't surprise me. There was almost a sense of relief that the drama of follow-up exams twice a year was over. The cancer had finally happened. No more wondering, no more anxiety about "if" or "when," no more dread that I would need another dehumanizing stereotactic biopsy.

Faster than I could say my name or take my insurance card out of my wallet, I was submerged into the System. My appointment book became filled with doctors' visits, business cards, who to call if this or this or this should happen, MRIs, CT scans, blood work, x-rays, and on and on. Cancer treatment was beginning to look like a full-time job.

---

45 Gary Stix, "World-Class (and Free) Heart Surgery in the Sudan: An Interview with Gino Strada," http://blogs.scientificamerican.com/talking-back/world-class-and-free-heart-surgery-in-the-sudan-an-interview-with-gino-strada/ (accessed January 6, 2016).

I had a medical oncologist; I had a surgical oncologist; I had a nurse I could call 24/7 with questions. My breast cancer was serious and it was also part of Big Business. In the world of commerce, I was a consumer, albeit a relatively uninformed one, and I was going to be a *big* one.

Over the course of my year of treatment, my guesstimate is that my cancer cost nearly a quarter of a million dollars. I don't have exact figures; I do know that each of my six chemos cost between $15,000 and $16,000, and the follow-up shot of Neulasta, a white-blood-cell booster, which I was given exactly twenty-four hours after each treatment, cost $6,000. These figures are what the hospital charged the insurance company and the total cost of those two items alone added up to $132,000. What this didn't include was all my doctors' visits, my mastectomy, my surgeries, *all* the other drugs, and the tests.

At the time of my treatment, most of the billing was paperless, so I saw few invoices and the insurance company took care of everything. This didn't seem terribly responsible to me—how could I be a conscientious consumer if I never knew what anything cost? True confession: as the faithful daughter of a man who suffered unspeakable poverty during the depression, I've been known to comparison shop for toilet paper. If I was going to spend a quarter of a million dollars on anything else, I'd make sure to do research, keep records, pay attention. Why should the medical field be any different?

My first visit with my medical oncologist lasted more than an hour. My husband came with me, and we were both grateful for the amount of time the doctor spent with us answering every question, viewing none as too trivial. She was informed, thorough, and kind as she walked us through this foreign land whose language easily tied our tongues into knots as we tried to converse with her. Everything seemed unfamiliar and complicated.

I remember hearing a question emerge from my own brain. "Has anyone done a cost-benefit analysis of this treatment?" It was one of the cartoon-like moments where all the dialogue is in neatly drawn white balloons. I didn't know I would ask that question; it must have been the cartoonist's idea, certainly not mine. Where had it come from? Who had asked it? I had no idea. I wanted to turn around to see who the crazy person behind me was who'd been so bold. Of course, I knew no one would be there—it had come out of my own mouth. I was both stunned and shocked, and so was my doctor. We skipped over that moment as fast as Peter Rabbit had adroitly hopped away from Mr. McGregor's wrath.

Cost-benefit analysis? Really?

Our appointment concluded with the doctor making sure that she handed both of us boxes of thin, white rubber gloves. My husband's were size large, mine size small—they'd thought of everything at the cancer center. So toxic would the chemicals used to treat my cancer be to our skin, she wisely cautioned us that we never touch anything that might come out of my body for a full forty-eight hours after a treatment. That made me wonder what they were doing to the rest of me—a thought that wasn't the least bit comforting. It was hard to find much gratitude for the gloves and the warning that went with them.

Nearly nine years later, the question about cost/benefit has haunted me. I've pondered how it was that I came to ask it. The question has become a game-changer in the way I viewed our vast medical structure. I began to doubt its stability—perhaps this was not a house built of brick after all, but hastily cobbled together with straw. I realized that my insurance premiums would never be able to keep up with the cost of my treatment. I calculated that it would take almost thirty-four years to reach the break-even point, where what the insurance company paid for my treatment equaled what I had paid the insurance company in premiums. The math was pretty straightforward. Premiums have increased accordingly; no insurance company bills itself as a charity. In 2005, my monthly premium was about $600, with little or no deductible initially. Today, should health issues force us to spend the full annual deductible, it would cost me $1,600 per month to meet my medical bills. As a spiritual director, my gross annual income averages $18,000, or $1,500 per month. The burden is staggering and I am thankful I'm not the primary income earner in my family. And while these are rough estimates, they give a sense of the monumental struggles between personal finances and the medical/insurance system.

The money issues are huge, hot, inflammatory; they have no easy solutions. Just think back to the furor Sarah Palin's comments about "death panels" raised in 2009 to understand this. Top that with the fact that, in 2011, Medicare spending reached close to $554 billion, 21 percent of the total spent on U.S. health care in that year. Of that $554 billion, Medicare spent 28 percent, or about $170 billion, on patients' last six months of life.[46] It's entirely possible that my odd question was fueled by my dim awareness about this side of the medical system.

Cost-benefit analysis concerns aside, I entered the medical morass with some measure of hesitation. I wasn't sure I wanted to do chemotherapy; it didn't make complete sense to allow into my system toxic chemicals that eventually made me so sick I didn't understand how it was that I *wasn't* dead.

During my treatment, I read an article describing how clinical trials for new drugs are generally conducted. The drug company first

46 Jason Millman, "It's Time to Bury the 'Death Panel' Myth for Good. Is This the Way to Do It?," *The Washington Post* (September 17, 2014), https://www.washingtonpost.com/news/wonk/wp/2014/09/17/its-time-to-bury-the-death-panel-myth-for-good-is-this-the-way-to-do-it/ (accessed January 6, 2016).

needs to find a population that fit the criteria—they had the disease for which the drug was being designed. This population sample was skewed in several ways. Without equal representation economically or racially, often the poor were too poor to participate. Plus, the clinicians seek the "healthiest" sick people—practically speaking, patients must be healthy enough to complete the study. It wouldn't help the trial if people died or had to drop out because the treatment protocol made them too sick. But once the drug is approved, it's released into the general population of the sick, with side effects that are often more severe than reported during the controlled study.

At that point, Neulasta was one of the newer medications on the market, designed to boost the number of certain infection-fighting white blood cells to prevent a serious infection on top of the cancer. Television was filled with Neulasta ads featuring bright, healthy-looking folks all proclaiming, "I'm ready to start." Big smiles all around as they declared, "Neulasta is going to help me with the side effects." Screen after screen of these impeccably dressed actors and actresses looked more like they were getting ready to go away for a well-deserved vacation rather than preparing to endure months of chemotherapy.

The truth is, Neulasta is known to give a patient "mild to moderate" bone pain. By the time my pain had reached its crescendo, it was so severe that the weight of my clothes was more than I could bear. I really did want to be dead and couldn't believe I wasn't. On one website, a woman described her Neulasta-related pain as "a 10+ on the 'screamer scale.'" I was relatively healthy when I started my chemo regime; even so I found the side effects of the Neulasta to be incredibly debilitating. I was confined to the couch for forty-eight hours, waiting for the side effects to subside. Then I needed twenty-four hours to recover from the exhaustion of the unrelenting pain.

When I was finished with the chemotherapy, I decided to ask my husband how these four months had been for him. I wasn't expecting much of an answer. At that moment I was just filling air space in the manner that couples who have lived with each other a long time often do. Not much going on, the room is quiet, just want to say *something*.

"So, Jorg, it's over!" Was my bald-headed self proclaiming some sort of odd victory? I wasn't sure. I didn't have eyebrows that I could lift to support my proclamation; no eyelashes that I could try to seductively bat at him; my yellowish "chemo-tan" completed the look. "Was it as bad as you thought it would be, easier, or about what you expected?"

He grew suddenly somber, to my surprise. "Oh, it was much worse." A man of few words, he felt no need to elaborate. I was stunned by his tone, and I knew he was responding at a much more serious level than the one from which I'd asked the question. I switched gears, glad that my years as a spiritual director had trained me so well.

"Worse? In what way?" I asked, curious, longing to keep the conversation going.

"Oh, it was much harder to watch you suffer than I ever imagined it would be." He stood silently by me and a tidal wave of tears began to build up in my heart.

"Oh, honey, I am so sorry. I am so, so sorry." If a voice could turn into a river of agony instantaneously, mine had, glistening, choppy, white-capped and unsettled. My sorrow was not an apology; rather, an expression of complete understanding, compassion, and deep sadness for these eighteen weeks of his silent suffering.

This conversation I'd so innocently started had jettisoned us into territory where no words were adequate or even necessary. Our hearts were suddenly, almost violently, exposed to the intense rawness that this experience of chemotherapy had been. Hugs were the clear answer, tenderly and generously given; our love the salve, the balm, the bandage we both desperately needed without even knowing that we did. This moment with him had an enormous impact on my relationship and regard for chemotherapy. If I had been hesitant at the beginning of my treatment, I was becoming convinced that I would and could never choose it again. The benefits did not exceed the costs on any level or by any standard, at least not for me.

In October 2013, I was diagnosed with advanced primary adeno-carcinoma with lepidic features in all the lobes of both of my lungs. Fatal. In an instant, my path became clearly illuminated: from feeling relatively healthy, vital, and active to sick, dying, dead. The irony is that I was a non-smoker. However, I'd been raised in a home where both parents smoked between two and three packs of cigarettes a day, placing me in a more vulnerable position for developing lung cancer. Some studies indicate that the chemotherapy I'd received for my breast cancer also has some negative effects on the lungs. Under close scrutiny, no other factors in my own personal health history or environment seemed to be present that would have caused this cancer.

Once diagnosed, I felt I needed to learn as much as I could about this disease and about how my lungs actually worked. Lung cancer accounts for about 13 percent of all new cancers. The estimate for 2015 is that about 221,200 new cases of lung cancer (115,610 in men and 105,590 in women) will be identified; it accounts for about 27 percent of all cancer deaths and is by far *the leading cause of cancer death* among both men and women. Each year, more people die of lung cancer than of colon, breast, and prostate cancers combined.[47]

---

47 "What Are the Key Statistics About Lung Cancer?," American Cancer Society, http://www.cancer.org/cancer/lungcancer-non-smallcell/detailedguide/non-small-cell-lung-cancer-key-statistics (accessed January 6, 2016.

The cost of lung cancer treatment during the last year of life for a woman who is over sixty-five years of age at the time of diagnosis is $92,524.[48] The numbers surprised me and left me pondering why fund-raising efforts for breast cancer are so much more developed and widespread. We can now buy almost anything pink with the promise that part of that cost will be donated to support breast cancer research.

I was curious to know if a color was associated with lung cancer—turns out the lung cancer color is white, and lung cancer awareness month happens in November. I discovered many websites; this one was at the top of the search window: http://www.choosehope.com/category/lung-cancer-clear-white. They enthusiastically promote what they are selling:

> *Choose Hope products are designed and created to provide humor, inspiration, and strength for lung cancer survivors and their family and friends. Choose from wristbands, car magnets, bracelets, caps and much more. Take advantage of Bulk Pricing on many of our most popular items . . . great for benefits, fundraisers, or giveaways!*

Make no mistake, the world of cancer—no matter the type—*is* Big Business.

Though I had breast cancer, I still found myself clinging tenaciously to the image of myself as a relatively healthy, active woman who took good care of herself. The prognosis for this type of lung cancer and stage is eight months *with treatment*. I'm not a statistician, but I understood this to mean that eight months after diagnosis, half of the

48 "Cancer Prevalence and Cost of Care Projections: Annualized Mean Net Costs of Care," National Cancer Institute, http://costprojections.cancer.gov/annual.costs.html (accessed January 6, 2016).

people are dead. At sixty-two, I hadn't expected this to be my end. When we went to the doctor's office to receive the news that was so apparent from my recent CT scan, the doctor's first question was, "So, what do you want to do and where do you want to go?" His tone was professional, clear, brief.

"Nothing." I replied. "I'm not going to do anything and I'm not going anywhere." I was equally clear and brief. As far as I was concerned, I had no need of further conversation.

His head jerked ever so slightly. As a prominent pulmonologist for more than thirty years, he'd seen and heard it all; he'd learned how to lean into the protection his professional experience had given him. I'd learned to do the same thing in spiritual direction. We don't help those we are serving if we're falling apart in front of them. If this was hard and painful for him, he concealed it. His focus as a healer was on me, his care as transparent as a clear mountain stream. He wasn't dispassionate. His professional manner became a necessary and secure container for all of us. I don't remember much more from that visit other than learning that my doctor did not believe in prognoses. I didn't leave his office with an idea that I had two, six, eight, or twenty-four months to cram everything into my life that I hadn't already done. My husband and I retreated to the safety of our car and took a few deep breaths. Unfortunately, this was, after all, not the first time we'd been in this situation. We were familiar with the drill.

First, call our daughters. Second, go to lunch. Let the news sink in. Let the news sink in? How in the world does one do this? Slowly. One tear at a time, one gasp at a time, one small loss of function at a time followed by another and another. And on. And on.

The choice to pursue no treatment other than alleviation of my symptoms (shortness of breath, chest pain, and cough) we nicknamed

Quality of Life, or "QOL" for short. Many of our friends and family pushed back, some gently, some not so much. Conversations would inevitably begin with, "Have you thought of . . ." or "Have you considered. . . ." I found myself wishing more people would applaud our decision. Thankfully, our daughters were behind us 100 percent. Our oldest, Amy, is convinced that, in a hundred years, we'll look back at this era of treating cancer with chemotherapy as dismally as we now do the era of leeches, among other old, touted treatments. Our younger daughter, Stacy, just kept chanting, "QOL, Mama, QOL," when I was ailing or feeling down. Although we didn't raise our daughters to become cheerleaders, they've become the best a mother could wish for.

Fortunately for me, my doctor stood firmly by my side. His own career and path were at a crossroads as he'd begun to seriously consider the spiritual side of medicine. His experience, training, and conditioning that all patients will choose treatment no matter what, even if it only "buys" them two months, was undergoing a significant transition. He quickly understood my choice and offered me only support and symptom treatment from that point. He knew only too well what chemotherapy would do to me and to my ailing lungs.

We agreed on monthly appointments, more frequent if needed, to follow the progression of the disease and to alleviate whatever symptoms were making me uncomfortable. One of the hardest parts of my choice to decline treatment was the sterile silence that followed my diagnosis, so different from my experience with breast cancer.

In this case, there was nothing. Every letter screamed at me in upper case letters: NOTHING. Not. One. Blessed. Thing. The silence of this space was not welcome, comforting, or sacred. The hole it created was more like what might happen should someone shove a foreign object into my eye. It actually *hurt*. It became almost more than I could bear. Raw, mocking, ragged, empty, painful, lonely—it felt oh, so very lonely. The absence of care created a caustic burn in my heart that I was desperate to assuage. I wanted to yell to the heavens, the stars, the universe, to anyone who would actually answer, "Is anybody there? I am *dying*. I am *dying* of lung cancer. Help! Someone throw me a life raft or jacket. Don't you want me to come in for a blood test at least? . . . Please?" But no one was there to respond to my pleas and my desperate tirades. No treatment meant exactly that: *no* treatment. My treatment "plan" turned into an experience that was corrosive and deafening. I was surprised. I was grateful it didn't shake my choice to only address the symptoms that would arise from the cancer itself. But wow, was it *hard*.

One of my most challenging conversations was with a dear friend who began our time together by telling me how sad she would be when I died. Her expression of sadness followed her long attempt to persuade me to look into chemotherapy, seek a second opinion, try alternative cures—anything to prolong my life or cure my cancer, no matter the cost. She and her husband had just listened to a story on one of the radio news channels about a thirty-four-year-old woman who'd been diagnosed with terminal lung cancer who'd been "cured." Wouldn't I want to look into it? How could I not?

After we parted company—it had been a *very* long lunch—I felt like someone had kicked me in the gut. I was surprised by the depth of my reaction because this was not the first of these conversations I'd had. I felt her loss, her pain, her frustration, her anger with me more acutely; her simple, unadorned honesty had stripped away my defenses. She hadn't resorted to using any of the "polite" niceties that usually pepper conversations like this. I was clearly unnerved. I did challenge her: "I think you're angry with me." I spoke gently and yet clearly; I did not want her to miss what I was saying.

That level of honest reflection proved to be too much for both of us. She responded quickly, almost from a place of feeling insulted. "I am *not* angry with you!" she replied. And that was the end of the conversation. We'd reached our capacity for truthfulness and soul-baring. My dis-ease that our words had spawned inside my heart lingered for several days.

I knew that her anger stemmed from the fact that I looked like I was doing "nothing." The part of me that still had doubts about the choices I'd made was waiting to pounce on me, adding to the already difficult conversation, berating, rebuking, and beating me up with the following familiar tape that should've worn out years ago: "Don't I realize that my friends and family are really, really sad, hurt, and upset? Don't I care enough, love them enough to do something? If I truly cared about them, I would be doing *something*. Doing *nothing* is just plain selfish." This voice never got tired of hearing itself spout its poison.

I was grateful that my doubts remained small even when those internal tapes became vociferous. I remained clear about my choices, supported by my immediate family, some friends, and my doctor. When I did worry—was I being selfish, egocentric, insensitive, or worse, unloving—it was usually the result of the conversation I'd had with my friend that awakened my doubts.

Even with a diagnosis of terminal lung cancer, treatment options abound and more are being aggressively pursued. There are set protocols for treatment, with the expectation that these avenues will "extend your life by two months." (Other sources, of course, provide different information and life extension is based on the patient's physical condition at the time of diagnosis, the type of therapy prescribed, and the patient's response to it.)

We can no longer ignore the reality—or live in isolation. We have, for many years now, been dancing around the rapidly growing reality that our lung cancer "community" is now global in scope. We're no longer scattered and separated by dirt roads that involve days of arduous travel to reach the closest neighborhood. Global Communities, modestly founded in 1952, has been one of the leaders in the movement to address need on a global community level. The Dalai Lama writes eloquently:

> *I believe that to meet the challenge of our times, human beings will have to develop a greater sense of universal responsibility. Each of us must learn to work not just for his or her self, family or nation, but for the benefit of all mankind. Universal responsibility is the real key to human survival. It is the best foundation for world peace, the equitable use of natural resources, and through concern for future generations, the proper care of the environment.*[49]

It is from within this context that I decided to write to my insurance company. I was inspired to do this by a segment of *60 Minutes* that aired on May 11, 2014. I hadn't watched the program in years, but it had been a long-standing part of our Sunday evening schedule while our children were growing up. We'd go to my in-laws' home on Sunday afternoon, eat dinner, then faithfully watch the show. The kitchen-duty people would rush through their chores so that they could catch at least some of this program that had become one of our favorites. Once my in-laws died, we simply stopped watching. We'd unconsciously abandoned this beloved pattern with relief—no big "meetings" or con-

49 His Holiness the 14th Dalai Lama of Tibet, "The Global Community," http://www.dalailama.com/messages/world-peace/the-global-community (accessed January 6, 2016).

versations; no turning off the TV in anger. It had simply become too painful.

I'm not sure what prompted me that spring evening to turn to that television channel; I have to assume something greater was at work in my life because the show did change my life. The story was about Dr. Gino Strada, who was, at the time of the show's airing, performing somewhere around 1,500 mitral valve replacements on children between the ages of fifteen and twenty-one in Sudan. These children had all suffered from rheumatic fever as a result of strep throat, which left their heart valves damaged. These "minor" diseases are completely treatable and curable, but the treatment and cure have been unavailable to this poorest of populations. According to Dr. Strada,

> *Rheumatic fever is becoming the leading cause of death in Africa and cardiovascular disease, according to WHO (World Health Organization), will become the leading cause of death in a very few years in Africa. The link to poverty is very clear. The WHO estimates that there are 20 million people with rheumatic fever in Africa. They require two million hospitalizations each year. There are five million people in need of heart surgery because of that. There are 300,000 deaths every year, two thirds of these deaths are children and children below the age of 13.*[50]

The cost of one heart valve replacement in the hospital in the Salam Centre (located on the outskirts of Khartoum, Sudan) is approximately U.S. $2,700 based on figures obtained in May 2014. The center relies

50 Gary Stix, "World-Class (and Free) Heart Surgery in the Sudan: An Interview with Gino Strada," http://blogs.scientificamerican.com/talking-back/world-class-and-free-heart-surgery-in-the-sudan-an-interview-with-gino-strada/ (accessed January 6, 2016).

on donations; funding is always a challenge. I have wanted to address this situation with my health insurance company. Friends I have shared my dream with have tried to dissuade me, convinced that the company would never agree to such a preposterous, ridiculous proposition. Why waste the precious time I have left? To each of my naysayers, I have responded, "One word at a time, one letter, one voice. It can't hurt." However, to date, I haven't sent the letter directly to them. I pray to be compassionate with myself as my nerve and the courage I need to send it seem to be vanishing as quickly as my breath. This is as far as I've gotten:

Dear Insurance Company,

I want to be honest with you. I do know (as I know that you and your hard-working actuaries also know) that I still have many years of premiums to pay you before you "break even" for what you had to shell out for my breast cancer treatment. I am in the "hole" big time. Good thing the insurance structure doesn't work that way . . .

I recently happened to watch a segment of 60 Minutes that featured a heart surgeon, Dr. Gino Strada, who is performing upwards of 1,500 mitral valve replacements for dying children in the Sudan. He charges them nothing. In May of 2014, this cost U.S. $2,700 per surgery.

In October 2013, I was diagnosed with "advanced pulmonary adenocarcinoma with lepidic features." At sixty-three, I am dying. There is no cure. However, there are myriad "palliative" treatments that I could choose if I were so inclined. Treatment might, according to what I have read, extend my life by two months and cost upwards of $100,000.

For many reasons, I have chosen to simply treat my symptoms as they arise so that I can maintain as much quality of life as possible given how poorly my lungs are performing. I am one of the "lucky" ones—as I write this letter to you, I am more than eight months past my diagnosis date, and I am still functioning independently. I know this puts me on the far right side of the bell curve, and it seems that my decline has chosen to be much slower than the average. I also plan to embrace death with dignity, so I will not decline to the point that I require extensive, expensive care.

Therefore, I am writing to request that you send the amount of money you would be paying for my treatment to Dr. Strada and his team. Let's start with a ballpark figure of $100,000. I know you have complex, indecipherable formulas that establish discounts for every item; let's just say the average discount is 25%. That brings the total to $75,000. Then we figure in my deductible, which is $12,700. We'll estimate that my husband's medical care for this calendar year uses $2,700 of that amount. That leaves $10,000 that I am paying for my care this year, and the balance that you pay is $65,000. This feels conservative to me and also workable.

I also know that this is a drop in the bucket—it will only cover twenty-four operations, but still. What happens when I consider twenty-four operations? I see twenty-four lives, and I see twenty-four adolescents in classrooms, heads bent over schoolwork. Or twenty-four healthy kids running in the street, kicking a soccer ball from one side to the other. I see twenty-four children with their families: Healthy. Happy. WELL. I would be foolish to think that this could start a trend of some sort, but I, too, am entitled to dream.

I completely embrace the philosophy of Martin Luther King and ask you to consider doing the same: He said,

> The universe is so structured that things do not work out rightly if men are not diligent in their concern for others. The self cannot be self without other selves. I cannot reach fulfillment without thou . . . All life is interrelated. All men are caught in an inescapable network of mutuality, tied in a single garment of destiny.[51]

I ask, humble and hopeful of heart, and with compassion for these children and their families who are living in such poverty in Africa. I beseech you from my own personal faith stance and prayer:

> Death is not something to fear; nor is it a mistake or a failure. It is the natural completion of my life, of all life, its second bookend. My heart's desire is to share whatever financial resources are available to me through my health insurance company with my less fortunate African brothers and sisters. My soul's path has helped me to make the following plea:

I ask: PLEASE send this money that you would not deny me had I chosen the usual path of active treatment until I die to:

---

51 Martin Luther King Jr., "The Ethical Demands for Integration," a speech given at a church conference in Nashville, Tenn., December 27, 1962 as printed in *A Testament of Hope: The Essential Writings and Speeches of Martin Luther King, Jr.*, James Melvin Washington, ed. (San Francisco: HarperSan-Francisco, 1991), 122.

Dr. Geno Strada
C/o EMERGENCY USA
San Francisco, CA
info@emergencyusa.org

This act on your part will make my death even more meaningful.
Thanking you in advance for your cooperation and understanding,

I remain gratefully yours,
Susan S. Jorgensen

PART TWO

The Other Side of Home

THIRTEEN

Reflections

Being born is like becoming a beautiful book. Of course, my book came from my mother; books of this sort usually do. Its initially empty pages were the softest cream color, smooth and satisfying under my fingertips, like one might imagine paper to be if it were finest suede. The thickness of the paper was precisely perfect for receiving a pen with a broad tip filled with ink the color of night, or for holding watercolor paints.

The cover of the book was calfskin leather, the color of umber, the corners softly rounded and simply, yet elegantly, embossed with a floral design. It had several thin, colorful ribbons that could easily return me to important spots, transitions, things I wanted to read or reread, places I wanted to etch even more finely into memory.

Over time, the book became filled with extraneous things—pieces of paper yellowed by fingertip oil, their edges tattered from being reread and refolded; locks of children's hair carefully saved from first haircuts, cards, notes, mementos as precious as the contents of a safe deposit box. After a while, the binding strained under the pressure of it all, pushed to its limit, an eight-month pregnant belly stretched taut and bulging with its contents, a joy to hold and peruse.

The haphazardly precious collection that was the book that had once been me began to fall away. The end wasn't sudden, but my lack of anticipation made it feel that way. The treasures that had been tucked carefully in there for safekeeping, for loving and cherishing, began to vanish as completely as trails of smoke on a gusty day. One by one. The precious contents of my life that had been coming together for more than sixty years became frantic, frenzied birds heading south and there was little time to look back or ponder.

My spiritual direction practice. Snorkeling. Hiking. Gardening. Flying up a flight of stairs just for the simple joy of exercise. Blowing my nose—who knew that annoying task took so much breath? Blowing out thick-wicked candles. "Graduating" to thin-wicked candles. Walking uphill. "Graduating" to walking on the flat. Deep belly laughs became smaller ones. Talking became whispering. Soon even the act of breathing was in jeopardy. Putting my beloved twelve-year-old Saab on Craigslist. Some days I thought I was fairly successful in imagining that everything was as it had been, but my body became my most reliable reality check because it lacked the ability to lie about *anything*. My mental contortions to bring me back to my "old life" before I was actively dying lacked any foundation in what was real and true. It was merely a pretense, as hollow as an egg that had been blown out and as lasting as a dust mote dancing in the air.

The book was thinner and I was powerless to stop its diminishment. All I could do was watch, bear witness, mourn, lament. The binding was no longer straining under its collection. Just the pages remained. And then, more slowly, the writing in the book began to vanish, to fade. Not all at once. Certain pages remained alive, some vibrant with watercolors and pencil, some neatly inked and spilling over with printed word. Others could only be read if you squinted hard under a bright light.

And then, of course, the binding began to give way and no longer could it hold its pages tight. The glue that had held and joined each page had begun to yellow, crack and fall away, dried up and brittle like browned leaves at the end of the fall season. Any slight disturbance, even a gentle jostle by an unaware passerby, would cause pages to loosen and then separate, drifting to the ground, pulverized footfall by footfall into dust and dirt, mud and stone. Some were caught up by a gust of wind. Scattered to the treetops and beyond, up, up the pages went until they no longer cast a shadow, no longer could be seen against the deep blue of the sky.

Slimmer. Slighter. Feeble-looking. The book was becoming lean and spare. There was no need to pick it up so often because so little remained inside. It seemed that, along with its treasures and its carefully crafted words and drawings, it had lost some of its authority. Sadness hung around it like musty old drapes, grief the tattered sashes that held them back. Not all the pages had even been written yet; they'd been judiciously (or now foolishly) saved for some unknown year in a future that would never materialize.

As the ravages of my disease continued their General Sherman march through my lungs, the book hardly recognized itself anymore. And while its actual physical dimensions remained the same—it was still a nine-by-twelve-inch book—it was no longer capable of occupying a prominent space on a coffee table. Once all the pages had fallen out, it would be a simple enough task to stick it under a pile of newspapers and forget about it. Not on purpose, mind you. It would just happen because the more pressing matters of the day would take hold; the world would move on quickly, propelled by the unseen forces that are always straining toward tomorrow.

And the hands that had touched this book, read it, cried and laughed over its contents, treasured it, left the notes and mementos, the paper trinkets—pretty soon they'd disappear, too. And then there would be nothing. No thing. Just empty space. No memory. No legacy. No collection. No recollection. Everything is, after all, in some fashion, radically insignificant, ashes to ashes, dust to dust. My irrational mind would not sugarcoat one random thought, one wild idea, one crazed image.

Initially, this was what it felt like to die little by little, day by day. I just kept getting smaller and smaller and smaller. Often the changes were numbing, like being thrust into a commercial walk-in freezer. When I was small enough, just like those pages shimmying their way into the heavens, I'd cast no shadow either. I see myself slowly vanishing before my very eyes. Soon, there will be nothing left of me. Nothing. Left. Of me.

It is thus that I found myself thrust—almost without mercy— into the *other* side of home. The second bookend was heavy, fraught with the unknown, but not malevolent, although some days I feared so. Who was I? Day to day it was changing. Who was I becoming? Besides smaller and smaller. Less and less active. Those changes were obvious.

At one point, I confided in a friend, "It would be so helpful if I could go away by myself for awhile. I don't know who I am as a dying woman." Swallowing hard, I voiced my greatest fear, "What if I don't like myself anymore?"

For nearly twenty-five years, I'd been making a silent retreat for eight days during the third week of November. These last eighteen years, I'd spent those days in a tiny cabin on the edge of a deep wood that was part of Still Point Interfaith Retreat Center. As the years went by, these days had become more and more simple. I brought all my food. I didn't turn on any electrical devices—no computer, no phone, no iPad, no iPod. I never got into my car. The silence provided the most exquisite music I'd ever heard. I wanted nothing to become a distraction between my soul and the soul of the Holy; annually, unadorned as every tree limb, I needed to face my own insignificance without apology or excuse. I knew a retreat like that wasn't possible, perhaps ever again. The lung cancer was becoming more and more a part of me and I was now too weak to spend eight days in a cabin. How was dying changing me? I felt differently and I wasn't able to articulate the "what" of that difference.

I'd gone through the same thing after I finished my treatment for breast cancer. Many of those changes were physical; at least those were the easiest to see and perhaps to accept. One day, not long after my mastectomy, I remember standing before the mirror in the half-bath on the first floor of our home, just off the kitchen and across from the door to our deck. My eyes darted everywhere, unable to rest, unable to settle. I would've been less surprised to find an image like Munch's "Scream" looking back at me than at what I did see; less surprised to find one of Dali's skulls, bleached white, casually tossed, the rest of the carcass buried in the dull, even-colored sand. Sadly, the person looking back at me was a stranger—completely bald; eyes dull and lifeless; flat, flaccid skin with a strange yellowish cast (those in the "know" called it "chemo-tan").

Where had I gone? More important and pressing, would I ever come back?

I was *so* tired. I'd weathered chemo, mastectomy, reconstructive surgery. I'd assumed that, once I'd cleared all three hurdles, I'd wake up miraculously healed and put back together again. I was. And I was not. I'd fallen into a black hole that was impossible to describe. It was fatigue. And it was not. It was depression. And it was not. It was some vague sense of disappointment. And it was not. As I stumbled awkwardly trying to describe what I was feeling to my oncologist, she suggested that I see the psychiatrist at the hospital.

"You'll like him," she said confidently. "He's just received a grant to study fatigue." I knew she was trying to help me. I wasn't sure I needed anything more than a little reassurance that what I was feeling was normal, but I didn't even know how to ask for that . . . I know I couldn't have anticipated what was laying in wait below the surface of my being.

More confused than desperate, I called the doctor.

My appointment time came. I had never met with a psychiatrist before—therapists, sure, but never a *shrink*. We began casually and I knew he was asking gentle questions that would help him find a diagnosis for what was ailing me.

"We're looking into the physiological and emotional causes for what we now recognize as 'chemo fatigue,'" he began explaining. His accent was thick and I had to listen very carefully to pick up every word.

I responded with concern, "I'm also very interested in the spiritual aspects of cancer and cancer treatment. Professionally, I am a spiritual director."

"Yes, well. We know that the physiological and emotional aspects of cancer and chemotherapy are related," he continued.

I wondered if the doctor had heard me. He had a pleasant enough manner and seemed to be genuine and sincere. Not one to be easily deterred, I pressed. "And how will you be looking at the spiritual aspects? I have some sense that what I am experiencing is related to the spiritual, but I'm having a hard time putting that into words. And I certainly don't know how to address this part. I feel separated from myself." My words surprised me—describing this to him at that moment was the clearest I'd been about the state of my being. It made ultimate sense: if I didn't know who I was any longer, how could I feel connected to me? I was grateful for the insight.

"Yes, well." These seemed to be his favorite words. "We are looking at studies that have explored both the physiological and emotional experiences of our cancer patients."

I was growing impatient. I knew it was important to mirror a client or patient's words back to them so they know that you have heard them. I decided to use the word "spiritual" one more time just to see if he would or could speak it back to me. I have always been fond of the "three strikes and you're out" rule. Suddenly it wasn't just a first-time consultation. I found myself, almost against my own will, on a fishing expedition. Would he take my bait?

"I understand that the physiological and the emotional aspects of cancer are very important, Doctor. As a spiritual director, I'm also trying to understand what is happening to me in terms of my own spiritual life and wellbeing." I was in distress. I wanted someone to hear me, to *really* hear me.

"Well, yes, the spiritual aspects are important, too." He nodded thoughtfully, although neither of us pursued it further. I was grateful that he finally had acknowledged this treasured part of my being. Clearly the study was not going to look at the spiritual, the aspect I was most interested in. Discouraged, I began to wonder if there would ever be room in the medical field—or anywhere—for the spiritual aspects of cancer and death.

I left his office disappointed; I also decided not to take part in the study. I so wanted to understand what was happening to me and I knew I couldn't treat myself. I was nearly paralyzed by the fear that I'd feel this way for the rest of my life. Statistics about chemo fatigue are not encouraging: after chemo, it's common for women to experience fatigue for six months or longer. I did recognize that it takes energy to grasp what felt like a sea shift in my identity, and I didn't have it. The issue I was facing also felt bigger, deeper, *bottomless*. Too much for the conversations I'd have monthly with my spiritual director. I wrote in my journal. I created calligraphy pages in an attempt to visualize the changes I'd undergone. Very little seemed to help. I kept coming back hollow, unfulfilled, reaped, a cornfield after harvest—just a stumpy, stalky, sharp landscape that looked too painful to traverse.

I was approached by several retreat directors who knew that I'd been treated for breast cancer. They wanted to begin to offer weekend retreats for cancer "survivors" and they knew I was an experienced re-treat facilitator. I wondered if this would be more like the lame helping the lame; I wasn't sure I'd processed enough of my own experience to be able to be and to give what I felt these people deserved and need-ed. And it is *never* good practice to work your stuff out in front of an audience.

We calendared, planned, marketed fairly well. We had to cancel more than once because not enough people had signed up. I pondered several things: my own internal lack of readiness—having to cancel was one way I was being saved from myself and more importantly, others were being saved from my foibles. Secondly, the very thing that might have proved helpful to these cancer patients was one of the things I doubted they had energy for. During my treatment, I carefully spent my energy reserves attending to my spiritual direction practice, my home, my family, and the financial work I did for my husband's company. At the end of the day, my coin bank was pretty depleted. No regrets—I'd chosen my priorities prayerfully and consciously to honor my desire to align myself with the divine flow.

As time went on and I began to experience healing on many levels, I would recognize myself. It was a lightning bolt of connection—sudden, immediate, charged, coming without warning. I'd become immediately excited because I felt like me again, but almost as soon as the excitement would arise, the connection would disappear again. This happened for a number of months. Blah. Bland. Zap! Connection. Excitement. Break. Sad.

These seven steps happened frequently enough that I began to recognize their rhythm. At some level, even though it was fleeting, the sense of connecting to myself for even one brief shining moment—a shooting star in a vast, blackened, deserted sky—did bring me hope. As the months went on, that connection would sometimes last for several hours. Like the friends who loved Tinkerbell and clapped her back to life, I wanted desperately to believe. Like Eeyore, it was a challenge to hold onto that hope.

A year after my last chemotherapy treatment and my last reconstruction procedure, my husband and I went on our first vacation. Without knowing it, this time away was exactly what we both needed. I returned more fully and completely myself than I'd been in months. The week afforded both of us the time and space to take a collective, long, deep breath—our first since my cancer and his.

"I'm baaaack," I'd announce to myself, my voice an exclamation point in boldface on a blank white page, a grin as broad as a banana across my face. Not 100 percent. Not 95 percent. But close enough.

Several months later, I met a woman who'd had chemotherapy and surgery for breast cancer. Like me, she'd worked through her entire treatment plan. She seemed sad. I could see a wistful, grayish cloud suspended around her head as she explained that, in all those months, she had never been able to catch her breath; eventually she retired for a full year so that she could regain her energy. "It was just so debilitating," she explained, a look of concern and helplessness darkening her face.

"I know. I felt that same way. It was like I fell into a black hole of unknown origin or depth. A free fall into the abyss. I could still function but I just didn't feel like me. It was like a part of me went away . . . far, far away. I wasn't sure she would ever find her way home." My newfound words came slowly and reflectively. This was not a conversation to rush.

This woman felt like an answer to my heartfelt prayers. I'd finally found what I'd been looking for when I was interviewed for the chemo fatigue study—someone who could understand and knew what I had gone through. The bond was instant, such a surprise and tender meeting of simpatico souls.

"Yeah, I know." She nodded her head in agreement.

"Don't you wish that someone could have reassured you *even once* that you'd more than likely come out of it given time? Wouldn't that have made all the difference in the world? I was so afraid this was it for the rest of my life. For me, the worry was almost worse than the fatigue, or whatever it was." I was filled with gratitude for this woman's sudden presence in my life.

"Me, too. It would've helped to know that I was going to be OK. Half of it was worrying that I wasn't ever going to have my energy back."

"I knew no one could give me an ironclad guarantee. I wasn't looking for that, perhaps just a little more encouragement, some sense that what I was feeling was *normal* . . . ." My words stopped suddenly, derailed by unexpected sadness.

Later, struggling for words to describe the experience, I found myself talking to another colleague. "How could it be that my soul has become an aging apple core that someone has tossed casually behind a rock? How?"

I feared that my spirit had gotten lost in the desert of Ezekiel's dry bones and was languishing there. Try as I might, I couldn't follow God's lead and I'd lost my voice to speak Ezekiel's prophecy that would bring me *hope*, bring me back to life. Only in retrospect did I know that the trauma of my treatment had as much of an effect on my soul as it had had on my body: Desiccated. Shriveled. Shrunken. Withered. The words I'd been seeking for many long months mysteriously appeared, becoming the key that unlocked the door to my very small self-made prison.

I could now move around, confident that the freedom to explore would allow me to know myself anew. I could never go back to who I was. But my searching was surprisingly fruitful; it wasn't just a futile exercise of head-banging, although it felt like that many times. Conversations with my oncologist; (even) the ill-fated match with the psychiatrist; my journaling and calligraphy pages; and the chance encounter with a bright, warm, articulate woman gave me the *hope* that I would like the *new* me just as much.

What I was feeling with my terminal lung cancer, eight years later, was different from that. Yes, I was tired. Many days, I simply didn't feel good, although it was hard to put my finger on what felt "bad." A line from T. S. Eliot's poem "Ash Wednesday" was haunting me: *Teach us to care and not to care.*[51]

Somehow, it felt like my pending death was teaching me "not to care." There were days when I felt too sick to care. At least I think that was what was happening. It was the best diagnosis I could make.

51 T. S. Eliot, *Collected Poems, 1909–1962* (New York: Harcourt, Brace & World, 1991), 86.

Once again, my interior space was becoming unfamiliar and confusing. I was often overwhelmed by the simple tasks of day-to-day living. Do I climb the stairs to the second floor? Do I stay here, on the first floor? What is lost if I don't? What is lost if I do? How could these questions become one of my daily focal points after such an active life? Could I hold on tenderly to caring and also learn how to "not care" about everything so deeply and incontrovertibly before my cancer, before my dying forced that choice on me?

My biggest challenge seemed to be the presence and care of my friends. I have always been a caretaker and, reluctantly, as I've aged, I've acknowledged my role as healer. My mother became chronically ill when I was eight, and looking after people became as natural and normal as breathing and eating, and a source of pride. As my lung cancer progressed, I found I couldn't "take care" of them any longer, not that they were directly asking. My desire was to comfort them in the face of their loss of me. I wanted to know how they were doing, what was on their plate, how I could help them. My heart cried out silently, "I'm sorry my pending death has caused you this pain." From the day after my diagnosis, cards and notes poured in. Phone calls. E-mails. So much sadness layered between so many expressions of love. There was no dickering with the role reversal that was required of me, of all of us.

The second big thing that happened was that I began to realize, for the first time, that it takes *energy* to absorb love. I hadn't known that. I felt like one of those little plastic red and white bobbers that you attach to a fishing line. I was bobbing around in bighearted waves of love that kept washing over me and I wasn't able to absorb much of them. This shocked, surprised, and saddened me. A double loss had happened: I couldn't take care of my friends and family in the ways I'd come to cherish. And I also couldn't soak up all the love being lavished upon me.

However, the light slowly dawned. I'd made the mistake of falling into the big hole of "either/or" thinking. Either I took care of them or I didn't. Either I absorbed all their love or I didn't. I became my father with his frustrating and maddening 1950s black-and-white world. How often we would argue when I was a teenager—me desperate to have him adopt my messy gray process; him desperate to keep it simple—no doubt, no questioning, draw the line in the sand and make it rigid. I kept returning to Eliot's poem, and boom! Finally it hit me between the eyes. He had created a mandorla with that one simple line: Teach us to care and not to care.

With the vision of that mandorla, the tension in my inner world began to ease; I could sense space and relief. I was Columbus discovering a new world that was both: I could care and I could learn to not care.

The Mandorla of Moderation

OUTREACH	WITHDRAWAL
Teach us to care.	Teach us to not care.

At about that time, I began to notice a mindset emerge in myself and in my relationship with my husband that made no sense whatsoever. I knew I hadn't tried to manufacture it or make it happen. I think if I had, a miserable failure would have resulted. I watched powerlessly as activities I'd held dear for most of my life were taken away, stolen, lost, or broken. In spite of this devastation, two things began to occur simultaneously. First, things that had felt inconsequential became exquisitely important—the birds on our feeder, the shadows on our porch walls that the morning sun had so finely painted, my morning cup of hot tea, petting our kitten.

My last summer, I was able to recognize the song of the goldfinches. Our birdfeeder hung right outside our bedroom so, when I heard them singing their cheerful dawn welcome, my heart would call out a morning greeting to them, "Good morning, Mr. Goldfinch. Good morning, Mrs. Goldfinch." This small bond wouldn't bring about world peace or cure my cancer and I was still dying. However, the energy of this little hello would ripple out into the world spreading good energy. And that's how transformation begins—one word at a time, one gesture, one expression of love. So many things grabbed our attention that summer. Every connection immediately began to foster a sense of wellbeing, gratitude, largesse, and bounty. A dear friend of mine, drawing on the richness of the Italian language, calls God's generosity "the *abbondanza* of God." What began as a simple practice of saying to each other, "Today is a good day," became a deluge of joy and love, laughter and delight.

How could I possibly be *happy*? How could we realistically wake up every day with smiles on our faces, appreciating the warmth of being wrapped in each other's arms, our hearts now radio beacons beaming simple joy out into the world? We both asked each other this question time and time again. And we both *felt* the experience consistently and at a molecular level. This was not about changing the weekly marquee at the local movie theater—ho, hum—or the outdated garb of a storefront mannequin. These were transformations that resonated and reverberated through and through us. There was no rational sense to be made of this, none at all. I was dying. Rather than having our lives totally diminish, we bore witness to the increase of our contentment and gratitude.

We discovered that the daily rituals of our life were holding us faithfully and in good stead. Breakfast time again: cereal, blueberries, and juice for him; tea, toast, and juice for me. We treasured our dance between the mundane and the intimate. Sometimes reading Internet articles silently, sometimes sharing interesting little tidbits from the day's news or most outrageous headlines. Genuinely sad when his schedule (mine was so drastically reduced it didn't so much resemble a schedule as a flow by then) meant he had to leave early and we missed this meal together. Finishing up, reluctantly saying goodbye amidst hugs and kisses and good wishes for the day. This is how dying in the Jorgensen household began to look. *Every day.*

My daughters and I had had a similar experience after my son died. We had spent one full day installing a memorial garden for Matthew on our property. The day had a soft feel to it, a mid-spring drizzle had been bathing the earth on and off all day; the land, the physical exertion, and the contentment didn't feel of our own making. It was effortless and a pure gift.

Our youngest, Stacy, was so puzzled. She even asked, "How can we be happy right now, Mama? Matthew's dead. It doesn't feel OK."

"I know, my honey. It doesn't feel OK to me, either. It's weird—I even feel kind of guilty." Wow. True confessions tumbled out over dirt, shovels, and fertilizer; messy hands, buzzing mosquitoes, and honest sweat.

"Me, too, Mama; me, too." It felt so good to be able to be this honest with each other.

It began to dawn on me over time that what we were encountering was the sacred power of the mandorla once again. And Brian Jensen's words continued to echo their truth: "the mandorla is healing, restorative, integrative, rebirth, and 'a place of poetry . . . to remind us that there are links between the things we always thought of as opposites.'"

I drew inspiration from T. S. Eliot's poem "Ash Wednesday." "Teach us to sit still."[52] I needed Eliot's simple request now more than ever. My spirit had been so riled up and aggravated by all the losses that my lung cancer had precipitated. The seeming loss of my identity felt the worst—I was unnerved, off balance. I became the little girl on the high seat of the seesaw, my legs dangling as my spirit became desperate to find its ground again. Eliot's insights filled the crevasses that my soul searching had carved into my heart: the quieter I became, the more I could feel his words permeate my soul.

---

52 Ibid.

FOURTEEN

Dancing between the Thresholds

A thin place requires us to step from one world to another and that often means traveling to a place where we have less control and where the unpredictable becomes the means of discovery.
—Sylvia Maddox[53]

Providentially, in the midst of writing this chapter, I had a fascinating conversation with an intelligent man with a scientific background. I'm not even sure how we got on to the topic of the space-time continuum, except that it was meant to be. I was mostly lost when he began to talk, but I hung in there because our conversation intrigued me and I kept asking him questions. Little by little, I began to recognize certain ideas, or rather, I began to translate his scientific language into the language that I use—the language of soul. There was an "aha" moment when I exclaimed, "Tony! We're talking about the same things, just using different language subsets." My excitement was barely containable.

So we could talk about the fact that linear time is actually a misnomer, that it is rather a continuum. I found myself explaining to him what

53 Sylvia Maddox, "The Mystery of God: Where Can I Touch the Edge of Heaven?" explorefaith.org, http://www.explorefaith.org/mystery/mysteryThinPlaces.html (accessed January 3, 2016).

I knew—that thin space/places predate the Christian era, are embedded in the Celtic culture, and have been recognized for more than five thousand years. Dr. Leonora Tubbs Tisdale, professor of homiletics at Yale Divinity School, refers to it this way, "In thin places, boundaries of time and space fade away. There is no yesterday, today or tomorrow—only eternity stretching forth in a timeless continuum."[54] I could talk about "realms," "being," and of a "fourth dimension" and he could understand that from a physics point of view. Our conversation was a high note.

My experiences of death arise from and return in non-linear fashion to this realm, this dimension, this thin space. While many people experience these spaces as physical, my own sense of them is that they are made manifest and incorporate myriad events that form a sort of cosmic soup base. For example, writing this book propelled me into thin space where time and space no longer exist as separate entities. Engaging with that activity I'm caught up in a flow that is a great, wide, smooth, placidly moving river whose only content is that of love, which most easily expresses itself in my soul as awe and wonder. Gardening does the same. Hiking. Intimate conversations. Love. Calligraphy. Laughter. Eating. Like thin space itself, the list is only limited by my life experience. In 2010, Mary E. DeMuth wrote her memoir, titling it *Thin Places: A Memoir*. Here's how she describes them: "Thin places are snatches of holy ground, tucked into the corners of our world, where we might just catch a glimpse of eternity . . . They are aha moments, beautiful realizations. . . ."[55]

I've been aware of this realm since I was three. If I were to draw a picture of myself inhabiting this realm, one of my feet would be fully root-

54 Leonora Tubbs Tisdale, "Glimpsing Heaven in Thin Places," *Day 1*, November 2, 2008, http://day1.org/1117-glimpsing heaven in thin places (accessed January 7, 2016).
55 Mary E. DeMuth, *Thin Places: A Memoir* (Grand Rapids, MI: Zondervan, 2010), 11–12.

ed in the three-dimensional realm and the other would be secured in the fourth dimension or realm. My legs would be slightly splayed—the degree to which they are would indicate how balanced I am between the two and how much the two circles overlap to create the "mandorla" or sacred space in the middle. When the dimensions barely touch each other, I feel the tension, sometimes quite painfully. At that point in the illustration, my little stick figure would look as though it were close to losing its balance because my legs would be strained to the point to nearly separating from the rest of me; my hair would be wildly askew; my arms waving wildly, batting at some invisible force; and my eyes would be open wider than would be thought possible.

Mandorla of the Soul—Phase I

MATERIAL	SPIRITUAL
Three-Dimensional Realms	Fourth Dimensional Realm

My diagnosis of terminal lung cancer has brought these two realms closer together. The three-dimensional world and the "fourth" realm mingle and overlap more firmly and completely with each passing day. The movement of each realm more deeply into the other has felt natural, organic, sacred, whole. I believe that this realm exists to support us as we travel the passage of death.

As the overlap of the mandorla increases, it becomes harder to distinguish the two separate energies with which we began. The experience of unity—of the *all*—grows; healing all division until the material realms and the spiritual realm are seamlessly blended.

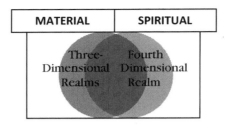

Mandorla of the Soul—Phase II

How does this space transform itself? Its ways are limitless, creative, mysterious, and very real. When we're afraid of death, when we resist, when we're desperate to live no matter the means or the cost, I think these ways are less accessible to us. Our sense of Life (Mandorla of Life) consists of the two overlapping circles of Birth and Death and the many, many mysteries held within that divine overlap. Our sense of Death (Mandorla of Death) consists of the two overlapping circles of Grief and Completion. Our senses are all compromised in the face of fear.

Mandorla of Life

BIRTH	DEATH
Beginning First Bookend	Ending Second Bookend

Mandorla of Death

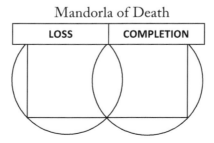

I've entitled this section "Dancing between the Thresholds," the thresholds being this three-dimensional world and the fourth realm. I wrote to a colleague recently to tell him of my lung cancer, saying, "Feeling deeply connected to that other realm that we know and don't know as the veil moves through its cycle of thins and thicks. It is much thinner now, and more consistently so."

His simple unadorned reply—"Could you please tell me about this other realm—the fourth realm? I'd like to learn of your relationship with that"—brought me to tears. One moment, I was enjoying our treasured morning ritual. The next moment, I was literally sobbing. So seldom do I receive an invitation to talk about this realm that my heart simply burst open like a fully ripened seed pod.

To share the simple experiences—to tell my stories—that I have so generously been given during this tender time since my diagnosis seems to be one way to offer a glimpse of the gifts that this realm holds for each of us. When death and we make that important turn, face each other, and begin our final approach toward each other, the love, the care, and the tender support will rise up to surround and generously enfold us. Each of us is given exactly what we need; our task is to open our hearts to receive. While my stories are unique to me, my sense is that they also contain the seed, the germ of the universal that will help you begin to open to your own. They are definitely there.

These are my stories.

੭ • ੮

My Grandmother Comes to Visit with Her Sisters

In the summer of 2011, my grandmother and two of her sisters came to visit me—not in a dream, although it was night and I was sleeping. So strong was their presence that I can only name it a visitation. When I awoke in the morning, I exclaimed to my husband, with delight, surprise, and perhaps with a bit of perplexity, "My grandmother, her sister Fran, and her sister Ett visited me in the night!" Their fourth sister, Polly, had died before I was born, and that seemed to be why she was missing. Thankfully, my husband is a most understanding man, and he's used to my "reports" from the "other side."

In this experience, the four of us found ourselves in the vestibule of a Catholic church; it was reminiscent of the church I belonged to for many years: a stone, gothic-style building, always a bit cold and yet very sacred—somehow, it seems to me that massive stones hold the holy in a way that little else does. My grandmother and her sisters had all been raised Methodists, although my aunt Fran had converted to Catholicism in the 1930s so that she could marry her Irish Catholic fiancé in a church. My first and only response to them, when I saw them standing primly side by side, was, "What in the world are the three of you doing in a Catholic church?" I didn't ask this question aloud. None of us spoke a word during the time we were together; there simply wasn't space in this realm for the spoken word, nor were words necessary.

They had all dressed carefully and respectfully in 1960-ish period clothing. Their outfits spoke for them—this visit was as important to them as I was. They had donned white gloves for the occasion, and their Sunday cotton lawn dresses were, while slightly faded, freshly laundered and pressed. Their handbags hung carefully from their wrists, and their stockings lay smoothly and run-free against their aging legs; their sensible, worn shoes were polished to a soft sheen. They were not the type for makeup, and their hats were simple pillbox affairs in the style of the day. They were prudent women, never flashy; they were practical and loving in an unmistakable and reserved manner that reflected their upbringing in a first-generation English household. They'd been orphaned shortly before adulthood and taken care of each other.

I stood in front of them. We were just gazing at each other. The smiles on their faces were hundred-watt ones—bright but not offensively so, spontaneous, stunning in their simplicity and lack of guile. After a bit, they began to fade, growing dimmer and dimmer. They stopped casting shadows and their bodies began to look more like see-through gauze than physical masses. Eventually they just disappeared from my sight. It was time for them to return to their realm and me to mine. I was intrigued. Why had they come? What was their point? Couldn't they have said something—*anything at all*—to me? Why didn't I ask? I knew it was because I was too surprised, and it felt safer to try to figure out why they were in a Catholic church, of all places, rather than to address them directly.

The more I pondered their visitation, the clearer and more beautiful it became. I realized I was being given the privilege of watching a talented artist complete a painting of the three of them. The more I contemplated them, the more sharply they came into focus and the finer the detail became. At one point, I noticed that my grandmother's gloves were slightly yellowed, that the netting on Ett's hat was slightly askew, and that the clasp on Fran's purse had opened. The only difference was that this was no painting—they were alive and well, come to visit me from the other side. I found myself being drawn into their experience of unabated, quiet joy. This was the gift they were hoping to convey to me. Not fancy. Not over the top. No bells and whistles. Just simple Joy. From simple women. The expressions on their faces spoke far more eloquently and explicitly than any words could have,

"We just want to give you a taste of what we experience here, as we are fully alive in this realm." I am reminded of the Shaker song written in 1848, "Simple Gifts:"

And when we find ourselves in the place just right,
'Twill be in the valley of love and delight. [56]

My grandmother remained close by my side during most of the rest of that summer. I still ponder their visit, fully two years before I was diagnosed with terminal lung cancer. I suspect that, in the realm in which they dwell, where linear time doesn't exist, they knew then what I only came to learn in October 2013—I was dying and they'd come to care for me as they had so beautifully cared for one another throughout their lives. The sense of joy they brought with them—their gift to me—remains as fresh and real today as it did when they visited me that summer night many years ago. I am deeply comforted by this space of love and delight that I know awaits me.

❧ • ☙

Samuel's Soul Speaks

Samuel was an elderly gentleman I visited regularly for a number of years, as he struggled with many health issues. In the end, diagnosed with acute leukemia, he was admitted to the hospital in grave distress. His heart at that point wouldn't tolerate any aggressive treatment, so his doctors recommended that he be brought home under the care of hospice.

I arrived at the hospital not long after he and his wife received the fatal news. They were clearly distraught and angry, and there was little I could do besides hold their hands and be as fully present as I could be.

Samuel was restless and fearful, railing against the heavens and

---

56 Joseph Brackett, "Simple Gifts,1848"

the unfairness that had been the theme of his life for many years. Why me? Why can't someone give me a break—just one—for a change? There was to be no comfort for this man. The love I could offer seemed less helpful than the finger-in-the-dike solution in a flood zone, trying to hold the entire ocean at bay. But it was all I had to give, and this frustrated me. Where was the magic wand when I needed it? I left reluctantly, heavy of heart, promising to visit their home in several days once hospice had established their routine and they felt somewhat settled.

I returned on Friday, ready to face the anger and restlessness once again. I had been praying for the grace to trust my love, that somehow it would be sufficient. I asked, too, for the grace to resist the longing to fix everything, to be the heroine, to save the day.

They had converted Samuel's study into his hospital room, the cumbersome bed just barely fitting. Even before I'd fully entered his room, I was taken aback, surprised, stunned by the change I could see and feel in him. He seemed even more shrunken than he had a mere four days before. The size of the hospital bed and all the medical equipment seemed like ignorant, impolite intruders intent on taking over the entire space, threatening to swallow him whole as they did so. I carefully made my way through tubes and wires to stand with him on the far side of his bed, the one away from the door. I thought this would make it easier for his family and caretakers to come and go.

Clearly, the most profound change in Samuel was that he was at peace. This was no fleeting peace—this was a peace that was like a firm, thick, soft white cloud into which you could sink and be held safe and secure. His eyes were closed, he appeared to be in a semi-conscious state, although he responded when I reached for his hand. His thin well-veined hand, its skin as thin as parchment, squeezed mine ever so slightly. What was more remarkable was what I "saw." I put this in quotation marks because this "seeing" is radically different from seeing with my two physical eyes, although I believe that these eyes are involved as well.

From the very center point of his crown chakra (the top of his head), I saw a large teardrop shape that sparkled and glistened, like glitter in a clear glass jar that has just been shaken, although the glitter wasn't falling because it didn't appear to be affected by gravity. Rather, it was dancing ever so gently, delicately, elegantly. I had to look closely to see the movement, and when I did, it was exquisite. The teardrop had definite shape, although I could see no border to it. I'm not sure what was holding its shape, only that the shape was clear, well defined, and sharp. It leaned back from his crown chakra at a forty-five-degree angle, attached by what appeared to be a single filament, a shimmering gossamer thread more delicate and beautiful than a single strand of a spider's web caught by a ray of sunlight.

I spoke softly to him, told him I loved him, and reassured him that he was going to be fine. And then, with difficulty, I told him that it was time for me to leave. We both knew that this was our final goodbye: we would not see each other again in this realm. I squeezed his hand, my gesture of farewell, and as I began to lessen my grip, he spoke. Or rather, I experienced his soul speaking to me. "He" whispered the words "thank you," I could see his mouth move slightly, although the sound seemed to come directly from his vocal cords. It also did not feel like his voice was speaking the words because of the effect they had on me. Those two common words, "thank you," felt like they permeated and penetrated every molecule of my being simultaneously with a beauty, a peace, and a presence that I've never experienced before. This was no human voice, at least not one I'd ever known or heard before this sacred moment. A slight tremor ran through my being as I realized that his soul and mine were communicating directly.

I bid the family goodbye with hugs and love and deep compassion and I walked out slowly to my car, clearly stunned, got into the car and drove the twenty miles home, all the while pondering the beauty of this dying man's soul and its intimate thank you to me. How blessed, how privileged I have been. Samuel died peacefully with his family by his side less than twenty-four hours later.

Thank you, Samuel, for revealing to me the gift of your soul's song and sparkle.

࿐ · ࿐

Crow Has Come

His arrival was simple and also surprising. He appeared at the end of February during one typical endless New England winter of snow and cold. I can't remember if he came in the early morning or the late evening hours. He arrived and entered during the thin time between waking and sleeping; his coming was both dramatic and reserved. The mysterious always seems to wear a cloak of paradox.

He stood in front of me, in full, elegant profile, between twelve and sixteen inches from my face, oriented to my left. I didn't see him arrive— one moment he was not there, the next he was. I could only conclude that he came in complete silence and was somehow, undetectably, made visible. How else to explain that I didn't see him come? Words and attempts at clear description miserably fail in this realm.

He was far enough away from me as to not threaten, close enough to capture my full attention. He was standing quite still, not a feather moving, not even the tiniest flicker to his eye, which held steady, fixed on some distant object that I couldn't see because Crow had filled my field of vision. So majestic was he, so suddenly had he appeared, I had no desire to see what he was seeing. I was completely absorbed by him and the mere act of being with him was sufficient.

Every molecule of his being was infused with dignified authority, understated certitude, noble confidence, pure presence, quiet power. He was a male peacock with no need to display his plumage. No need to speak, no need to engage my eye, no need to communicate through any means in any realm. His presence alone was enough to convey everything, every thing.

His bony legs and feet looked like he had affixed winter twigs to his body. He was on solid ground even though I couldn't see the object or earth upon which he'd landed. Whatever it was that held him securely didn't fall under my own limited ability to see; it was out of human range and nonetheless very real because Crow was not hovering. He was standing tall, attentive, erect, alert but not anxious. His beak was black as coal; his feathers equally black, but with a silky sheen and a complex texture. His finely shaped muscles rippled just the slightest bit and his eye was tiny with that speck of light that happens in the experience of reflection. There was nothing flat or dull about this bird.

The background surrounding him was an amazing blue color; nothing else was there. No striations, no patterns, no clouds, no miscellaneous objects or decorations that might distract my eyes from Crow. Just blue, blue, blue for as far as my eye could see, extending itself out into an endless panorama. Looking up color charts on the Internet, I discovered several websites that name it "deep sky blue"; it conveys the ability to express truth through the power of the spoken word. It wasn't a color created to soothe the eye; rather, it was vivid and clear, startlingly so. Crow stood out in bold relief, emanating from the other realm, this "fourth dimension," in a way that was intrepid, daring, and even audacious, but without any ego to entangle him.

And so I wondered: Why is Crow here? Clearly he is about the spoken word; he will definitely not be mute. It appears that He is in the same realm, on the same plane as my long-deceased dearest grandmother and her sisters Ett and Fran. This realm they inhabit is so close that I have the sense that I could reach through and actually touch all of them in those fleeting moments when the veil is at its thinnest.

I don't believe that Crow and my elders know each other in the sense of being friends or being aware of one another, even dimly. I am fairly certain that they don't see one another, at least not in the way that you and I would say we see each other. Even though I was curious about and intrigued by him, I promised myself (and without knowing it, him) that I wouldn't do any research about him until I'd written about his coming, until I'd asked him, "Crow, why are you here?"

Rather than fulfill my sincerely proclaimed promise, my mind busied itself for days with questions, questions, questions of no real consequence. Are you a crow or a raven? Really, what color are crows' beaks, because clearly this one has a black beak? How is it that I don't know this seemingly obvious and mundane piece of trivia anyway? If crows have yellow beaks, well then it can't be a crow, now can it? Then my mind began to ask the same thing of the raven. And I do know with certitude his beak was black. My rattling, prattling mind was like a loose marble careening aimlessly on a tile floor. The black and yellow debate about beak colors was noisy and riotous fun, and it served well as a distraction; my mind definitely prefers minutia to mystery.

Such is the nature of an inquisitive, busy brain when presented with something that lies beyond its ability to fully understand or even worse, when something brings it right to that sharp and jagged edge of the unfamiliar. Fear and loss of control become careless provocateurs that easily sabotage sane thought. When Crow appeared, my own mind became an anxious hamster on the wheel; 'round and 'round the animal fretfully traveled, hoping to disturb me long enough that I'd forget completely about this mysterious visitor.

Perhaps a week after Crow appeared, as I was in the kitchen preparing breakfast, freshly showered and still surrounded by the lingering gratitude of water and soap, warmth and skin, I heard him say, "I am guarding you." Hmmmm. I had no idea what that meant, and I wasn't really impressed. As is true of the deepest nature of mysteries that they do not or perhaps cannot reveal themselves all at once, he spoke again, "I am holding space for you."

My mind's immediate response was to aim hard questions to dissect—perhaps even pulverize—Crow's words. The strain to put Crow's response on a slide and examine it under a microscope for further knowledge and explanation nearly swept me under and out to sea as efficiently as a vigorous, high, full-moon tide would. Part of me needed to satisfactorily and summarily disperse the mystery of him.

A few days later, I was driving to work on yet another frigid winter's day. I found myself pondering how very blessed I've been by so many things, most especially to find myself accompanied during these tender days by Crow; my grandmother and her sisters; and my dear friend who died of AIDS in 1999, Aelred. Their spirits were engaged, like mine was, in a gentle rhythm, drifting closer to the Celtic thin spaces one day and then the next, out into a further realm. Our dances became our souls' lullabies.

My ponderings brought me to the inevitable question of "Why me? Why should I receive these profound blessings and insights? Why so much comfort for one little human being?" And then, the next layer of thought was about responsibility. Do these gifts require or seek payback? Carry obligations? My heart didn't resonate with any of these questions. My sense was that when a gift is given freely—truly freely—there is no expectation of anything. The gift is motivated by the sheer, simple joy of giving.

At the same time, my mind was gently probing this landscape. And that is when I heard these words from Crow, spoken quietly as a mantra, "Be the seed; be the seed; and one more time, be the seed." Not *become* the seed. Not *sow* the seed. *Be* the seed. We are all fertile seeds. We drip seeds from our pockets every time we move, think, sing, talk, dance, sit. Every time we breathe, seeds escape from our being, both good and bad, both wholesome and toxic.

In that moment, I knew I was coming to understand Crow, at least a little bit. On some level, in some realm yet to be charted by human hand, my soul was grasping Crow's counsel. With that, I could breathe more deeply, and settle into a natural and more graced level of rest. From that space, my heart could graciously extend the warm invitation to this magnificent being: "Welcome to my home." This seed began to flesh itself out— an incarnation was happening that was humbling, respectful, and so very reverent. I believe I was born carrying this seed, whose primary purpose is to support this emerging conversation about death: that it is necessary, essential, about completion and beauty.

Still, I'm left wondering about things for which I have no answers and I believe that this particular strand of wondering is important and has value. What has changed with the appearance of Crow? What is his significance? "Floating" since the date I received my cancer diagnosis—in a land that has no name and no linear timeframe—has presented clear challenges. It has been work to stave off the inevitable "when" questions. So, the appearance of Crow has made me curious and a little more aware? I pose this as a question.

Clearly for me, my heart opened to Crow's presence because some part of me is more ready for this next state of being, whatever it is, however and whenever it arrives. Otherwise, I don't believe he could have so effortlessly pierced the thin spaces of my being and entered my consciousness so clearly and vividly. Some part of me would have said, "No. Not yet."

And, equally clear for me is that the universe is also more ready for me. I find this exciting, curious, and unbearably sad for those who will miss me. It does feel that I've entered a new stage of this dying process. And, the danger at this point, or perhaps at any point in any conversation about death, is to draw conclusions. We have no hard data, really, even though we have many fascinating anecdotal tales gathered from near-death experiences. Any "conclusions" that we present about the dying process are more than likely to be faulty. We can only speak of what we know; beyond that, we have entered the wild world of speculation, which can be fun as long as we don't mistake it for hard truth. For me, I know that Crow has come. I know that my grandmother and her sisters have drawn close. Something in my own life's path has shifted. This is what I know. And it is enough. It is always enough.

I am grateful that Crow is guarding me, holding space for me, and has asked me to "be the seed." I am grateful and so honored to know that I'm called to be this particular seed, that its shape and purpose have been partially revealed to me. I am also grateful that my spirit guides, ancestors, and numinous companions are assembling faithfully. Together, we are traveling toward each other, preparing gently and tenderly and looking forward to an elegant crossing.

❧ • ☙

Death Canal and Womb

I'm also aware of how quickly the landscape changes in this Celtic thin space. The next change that happened seemed monumental. I was at my monthly meditation circle; the women gathered were chanting mindfully as the one who sat next to me was drumming the rhythm. With each beat, I could feel my membranes expand and contract; they had become the heart of the drum—steady, clear, strong. It was disconcerting to experience my tissues move in that way, yet somehow true and right. Sitting in silence after our chanting, I began to feel a shift that wasn't possible to name immediately. My brow furrowed with the effort of wanting to name what I was experiencing. At the same time, I tried to stay beneath the rumble of thought. Back and forth I bounced, a volleyball in play: "Shhh . . . quiet, meditate!" And then, incessant chatter: "What am I experiencing? What is this shift?" Because the question arose from a place of curiosity rather than fear, my mind was at peace.

Sinking back down into meditative space, I first heard the words "death canal," followed by the completion of the thought: "I am in the death canal now." The revelation was imbued with the sacred and I was grateful for the guidance and the name. Reflecting on this later, it seems logical that, as we each pass through a birth canal, we also pass through a death canal. I was explaining this to a friend of mine not long after that and I said that our births are all so unique and individual. While each person goes through a mother's birth canal and siblings go through the same canal, no two births are the same. The death canal feels much more universal.

"Do you see any lights?" she asked, to encourage my exploration of this new and unusual space.

"No, I don't." I answered thoughtfully. "And yet, it isn't dark, either. It's hard to describe the space. It's very soft, hushed, muted, gentle, quiet, and slow," I was wishing I could be more articulate.

She reassured me that my experience felt "right" to her. Such new territory for both of us, and I was grateful for her listening ear and fine support. Further reflection has refined my sense of this space. It appears to reverse the tripartite birth process, which moves from birth womb to birth canal and then out into the world in the way that most expresses and reflects a particular being's spirit. The death process moves from death canal to death womb to the soul's return. Meister Eckhart, a thirteenth-century Dominican mystic teacher and preacher, spoke often of the soul's *ausfliessen* and *durchbrechen*. Translated, the ausfliessen is the soul's flowing-out, which is completed by the soul's durchbrechen, or return. I'm taking liberties here when I ponder and posit that the soul's outflow is one way of referring to birth and the return one way of referring to death. Again, they complete each other structurally and energetically.

The death canal feels narrow and yet not constricted because the space is fluid and natural; it has a "give" to it. Our Being travels down this canal; I feel no discomfort or sense of being squeezed out of or into something into which I wouldn't fit. The movement ends at the soul's arrival in the death womb/tomb. For Christians, I wonder if this might correlate to Jesus' time in the tomb. The presence there is accommodating and woven with love and compassion. It provides everything a person's soul needs to complete its passage. Once passage through the canal is complete, we dwell inside the "death womb" until our souls are ready to receive and be received into space, "lovely, lovely space going on forever."[57] This process is consistent with what I've experienced with my mom, Mrs. Callahan, and Samuel.

❥ • ❦

Another Guide Appears

One night, not long after that, I found myself once again hovering in that boundless area between wakefulness and sleep, although this was at the threshold of the night. Three dark, hooded figures appeared hovering, silent, and watchful at the edges of my consciousness. Their soft, heavy hoods obscured their faces, although their eyes were picking up some distant light source—perhaps they were mirroring my own eyes, the source of the light emanating from within all of us. They appeared both ominous and not; I knew I was unfairly layering upon them my own experiences of dark, hooded figures, and I attempted to hold that interpretation at bay so they could reveal themselves freely, in their own time, as they would.

The next morning, I was describing the figures to my husband and I said, "They remind me of one of the cartoon characters from *Masters of the Universe*. Remember the little creature who hovered; he wore a red cape with a full, heavy hood, and you couldn't see his face? What was his name?"

"I have that little guy sitting on the ledge in my office," he replied. "Oh, what the heck was his name?"

We struggled and struggled, our tongues on the verge of twisting into intricate knots as we spouted out all sorts of sounds, laughing at the vagaries of old people trying to remember things.

---

57 Joel Levey and Michelle Levey, *The Fine Arts of Relaxation, Concentration and Meditation: Ancient Skills for Modern Minds* (Boston: Wisdom Publications, 2003), 179.

"He was with Skeletor," I sighed. "He was one of the bad guys," I spoke gloomily as I watched my dread nearly write itself off the page in bright red ink. To myself, I am thinking, "Oh, great, I'm doomed. I've got little dark beings intent on spreading evil, hovering at the edges of my consciousness."

Jorg pulls through at that very moment. "Or . . . Or . . . Orco!" The exclamation point at the end of the word emphasized one more memory victory that is just too sweet for words.

"Orca?"

"No, that's the island, Susie." He is patient with me, although I can almost hear the eye-rolling tone in his voice.

"Let's look him up on the Internet." Of course we spell his name wrong. We discover in our surfing that it's "Orko" with a "k." And he's one of the good guys from another planet, who, when he comes to the He-Man universe, loses his magic powers. He was a source of humor and comic relief in the first incarnation of the series in the 1980s. In an article I read on Wikipedia, he's described as "proven to be a good friend and a valuable ally," even though he's also quite inept at what he does. A humble, most accessible friend had been sent to me, a perfect companion because I know about ineptitude, friendship, allegiance, and above all, humor. A familiar, approachable friend in an unfamiliar land.

❧ • ☙

Angels?

My spiritual path hasn't given me much of an attraction to angels, or so I thought. It took a friend to point out what most of us miss when the forest gets too thick to see the trees. She would visit and inevitably mention her sense of angels around me and our home. Of course, I would refute every claim she made: "Angels don't work so much for me," I'd point out. Much to my chagrin, I was a bit haughty about it, too. She'd laugh, dismissing my mini-revolt with humor as would I; our playfulness was contagious. Perhaps we'd "caught" it from these angels who seemed to have been gathering around me for quite some time—a subversive lot if ever there was one.

The first indication that they were intentionally here was the sheer number of Willow Tree angels that many people in my spiritual direction practice had given me over the years as expressions of gratitude, love, and appreciation. Susan Lordi, who began the series in 2000, explained her vision, "The original inspiration for Willow Tree still holds true today: Willow Tree is an intimate, personal line of figurative sculptures representing qualities and sentiments that help us feel close to others, heal wounds, or treasure relationships."[58] Though they didn't reflect my own personal style as other things in our home did, I displayed every one; I couldn't part with any of them.

When I decided to write down my story about Mrs. Callahan, this angel presence suddenly took on a much more serious note. What remained long after the telling of that tale was the sound the wings of the angels continued to make. At that point, I'd written, "I 'saw' angels in diaphanous dress whose wings became a sacred instrument accompanying the heartbeat of the universe, hushed and rhythmic."

Many traditions practice sacred listening, in both external and internal environments. My first experience with this type of listening was spontaneous. In 1992, I awoke during the first week of Lent and "heard" one thousand orphans weeping in agony in my bloodstream. It

---

58 "The Willow Tree Story," Willow Tree, http://www.willowtree.com/wt-home-story/wt-home-story,default,pg.html?brandId=WT (accessed January 3, 2016).

was powerful, uncomfortable, irrefutable, and disturbing. Their haunting sound became an incarnational anguish, and I knew without doubt that this was the sound my soul was expressing during those forty days and forty nights of this season of penitence and fasting. The sound never left me. My soul became an intimate chamber orchestra pit filled with musicians intent on setting free the sacred tones from these orphans' mouths. And then, as quickly as they had begun, they concluded and my soul was returned to a welcome, blessed silence.

The intimate sound of the angel wings with which I'm participating right now is the same. I couldn't say that I'm simply "hearing" it because describing it that way is too passive. This sound involves the totality of everything and everyone in every realm. The only difference between the orphan and the angelic sounds is the melody. The angelic sound accompanying the heartbeat of the universe is stunningly beautiful and so very comforting to my soul as it continues to dance between these mystical, mysterious, half-revealed thresholds of the material and the spiritual. I can't predict the future; I have no idea how long this particular sound will remain. My invitation applies to the here and now. The sound speaks clearly: "Absorb this gift and allow it to nourish you as it will in this moment." And it is enough. As the poet Anne Alexander Bingham wrote, "It is enough to know that as long as there is a universe I am a part of it."[59]

$$\text{\textciterighthalf} \cdot \text{\textciterighthalf}$$

A Pedicurist Named "Matty"

Endings. I've written this book remaining faithful to a chronological order because it seemed to lend greater clarity to the narrative. It seems

59 Anne Alexander Bingham, "It Is Enough," as published on *The Writer's Almanac* by Garrison Keillor website, http://writersalmanac.publicradio.org/index.php?date=2014/01/22 (accessed January 4, 2016).

strange to end a book about death before I have died, and yet, the natural order of things would dictate that this is the only way it can happen. This final story took place more than eleven months after my terminal lung cancer diagnosis and most probably a full five years after the illness had become an active force in my cells. By the time this story happened, hospice had been taking exquisite care of me for almost a month and most health practitioners who were treating me had taken to calling me a "walking miracle." I didn't always feel that way; often the suffering took on the sheen of a curse rather than the blessing of a miracle. And at the same time, grace was every moment.

Providentially, this story coheres around synchronicity, one of Carl Jung's concepts. I went to Wikipedia and found the article on "Synchronicity" to describe the concept fairly well. I will leave it to you to delve deeper into this concept with the hope that you will experience your own bit of synchronicity.

My daughter was visiting and, as is often part of our regular outings, we were going to have pedicures. She is a much freer spirit than her mom. I always go to the *same* salon and I have my little card on which I've been building up points with each pedicure, waiting for the day when I accumulate enough to get something for free, although that day never had seemed to materialize.

That day, we officially appointed her the secretary; she was going to call and make our appointment. She started, "Come on, Mom, time to break out of the mold. We need to try something different. I'm going to call a salon we've never been to."

I groaned; my protests began immediately, so feeble that they wouldn't impress a mouse, and there she was, dialing the phone before my vote had even registered. We were both in good humor. We arrived and she helped me out of the car as I whispered, "So help me, babe, one bad vibe, and I'm out of here; we'll go to my regular place." We were both enjoying the playful haze of humor propelling us toward the door.

As we opened the door, I said to her, "You know, these will probably be our last pedicures." My voice caught because, for me, this is a raw truth that I hadn't meant to say, so I quickly corrected myself, "Our last pedicures *for the season*." After all, it *is* September in New England and sock weather is knocking on the door. That's the practical-speak. Emotionally, I've just built a safety cushion so that I can hear the deep-down truth of things. This was far more reality than I was prepared for on that sunny September morning and the exhalation of my breath became my shield and support.

As soon as we opened the door to the salon, we were greeted warmly by three women who'd emigrated from Central and South America. My salon experience to date had been limited to primarily Asian proprietors; I was immediately aware of the new energy. My pedicurist was warm, gracious, welcoming. *We* had made the exact right choice, or . . . even at that early moment at the beginning of my pedicure, I knew there were forces at work here that were far beyond little human beings to summon.

With those fateful words still ringing in my ears, "These will probably be our last pedicures," I decided to treat myself to the ultimate pedicure. I picked the polish, sat down, and my pedicurist began. Her energy was gentle and it felt like her spirit sank effortlessly into my tired feet and legs. I began to talk to her a little.

"What is your name?"

She smiled warmly, her dark hair clasped in a pony tail that swung as she smiled. Behind the deep darkness of her eyes, her soul was dancing tiny specks of light. "Matilda."

"Oh, what a lovely name." I was immediately enchanted by her accent.

"Yes, but it is so old-fashioned," she lamented. "My family and friends call me 'Matty.'"

I swallowed. Even though her massage had already begun to lull me to sleep, I didn't miss this synchronous moment for one second. When my son was born, we named him "Matthew." Everyone warned me, fingers wagging and heads shaking as they did, "Bad name. No one will call him that, Susie. They'll call him Matt or Matty. You'll be sorry."

I was determined, though; I loved the name and had been calling him that for the entire time he'd been growing in utero. It really didn't matter to me what anyone else called him. I would respond always, "People can call him what they want to. I'm going to call him Matthew. It's one of my favorite names." And so I did. And people called him "Matt." Or "Matty."

There we were. In a nail salon I'd never visited before, one I'd been quite determined not to go into. I was pretending to be a little ornery because the pretense was making us laugh, love, and have fun. I don't use the word "jovial" often, but a jovial mood had infiltrated the salon experience. Out of "Matty," my pedicurist, was pouring the most healing energy I've ever felt. Like the paraffin wax, it warmed my feet and legs and soaked in deeply. I found myself in a space that was neither here nor there, drifting between realms, dancing between thresholds.

My coterie has been quite the wild and surprising bunch of spirits, ancestors, four-leggeds, two-leggeds, and thousands of pinpoints of light: from my grandmother and her sisters, to Samuel's soul, to Crow, to the revelation of the death canal and womb, to Orko, to Susan Lordi's angels, to the angels around Mrs. Callahan, to perhaps the biggest surprise of them all—Matty the pedicurist.

Others will come as they are needed. Amen. Blessed Be.

GRACE IS EVERY MOMENT

Grace laughs!
With her head thrown back,
and her mouth wide open
out flow rivers of wonder,
waves of elation,
streams of pleasure.

She chortles and snorts,
cackles and chuckles.
She giggles and smiles,
titters and coos.
When you least expect it,
she will let out a great big raucous,
unrestrained, unconstrained
  belly laugh
that erupts from the bowels
  of the earth,
a volcano of joy.

Grace delights in being found.
She is an excited child
playing hide and seek
who hollers out
from behind the sofa,

"I'm over here!"
giggling as she does.
We overlook her. We forget her.
We lament and shake our fists
when we're sure we've lost her.
Ah! Grace!
Determined to be found,
Grace is never lost.

The gossamer threads of her
  presence
constantly cross the threshold
between here and there,
before and after;
between up and down,
in and out.
She wraps herself around us,
we the babe, she the swaddling
  clothes.

Grace is breath and light,
water and fire.
Grace is tears and trembling,
Music and dance.
Grace is every moment!

Epilogue

The sun does not shine in the tunnel of grief. I have been in this dark tunnel for six months now; it has been a hard journey so far. Susie is gone from my world but she remains in my heart. I tried to engineer my way out of the tunnel, but it is not a place that has an external solution; a significant jolt to my engineering mind. The passage through the grief tunnel is all arranged by the internal workings of the brain, not visible to me. There are no shortcuts. I do not know how long it will take, nor how fast I am progressing. I have had one good day in the past eight weeks or so. I remember that day because it felt so different; the sun was out and the birds were chirping. It took me a while to figure out what was so different—turned out it was, that I actually felt good. I hope there are more of these days on the way.

A bright spot in my life are the gardens that surround our house. Susie was a gifted gardener; she has left me a treasure. Although I am now in charge of them, I will always think of them as Susie's Gardens. We must be having really good garden weather this summer because they're doing well despite my inexpert attempts at care. But I find that the process makes me feel better. On most days I think that Susie would be pleased to see me in the gardens; on other days I sort of flinch because of what I see happening in parts of the garden and I think of what Susie would say to me.

Susie died in our home on December 29, 2014. Amy, Stacy, and I were at her side. Shortly after she died, Nora and Nancy came and washed and anointed her body. We then placed her in a burial shroud. After she was cremated, Amy and I went to her plant-potting bench on our deck and placed her ashes in an elegant urn that was made for her by Kathy, one of her clients, a gifted potter. The urn was the centerpiece for a twenty-four-hour vigil that was conducted at Nora's temple. We then had a memorial service at Lourdes of Litchfield. Amy picked the closing song; it had to be something by Laura Nyro. Susie needed a closing with some attitude. Amy picked "And When I Die," written by Laura Nyro and sung by David Clayton Thomas and Blood Sweat and Tears. As I sat in the pew, next to my brother Karl, the first few harmonica notes floated out of the speakers and I suddenly re-called what the first words would be: "I'm not scared of dying." When I heard the words, they hit me right in my heart. Susie was indeed not scared of dying. She faced her death with grace. She will remain in my heart forever.

Rob Jorgensen
July 2015